Personality Intelligence
MASTER THE ART OF BEING YOU

Personality Intelligence

MASTER THE ART OF BEING YOU

(For Your Sake and Everyone Else's)

Merrick Rosenberg

Take Flight Learning

Take Flight Learning

TakeFlightLearning.com

ChiefParrot@TakeFlightLearning.com

Softcover ISBN: 978-1-959554-31-8

Hardback ISBN: 978-1-959554-08-0

eBook ISBN: 978-1-959554-07-3

10 9 8 7 6 5 4 3 2 1

Printed in the United States of America

To all the amazing teachers who have walked with me on my journey—my parents, Sandra Brossman, and my senseis— I am forever grateful.

To Traci, Gavin, and Ben, you are the heart of my world.

And to Merlin, the original parrot, your magic lives on.

Acknowledgements

To my incredible team, thank you for your commitment to sharing the birds with the world. My life and this book would not be what they are without you.

A special thanks to Jeff Backal, Andy Kraus, and Beth Holt. You help turn the vision into reality.

I want to express my gratitude to the outstanding sales and marketing team at Take Flight Learning—Rick Kauffman, Jim Di Miero, Josh Levoff, Patrick Kelly, and Steven Farber. Your dedication to helping others experience the power of our work is what makes our reach so vast.

An enthusiastic Parrot thank you to all the certified trainers around the world who infuse their wit and wisdom into bringing the Eagles, Parrots, Doves, and Owls to life, especially Kerry Bayles and Jason Meucci.

A heartfelt thank you to the people behind the scenes at Take Flight Learning who deserve to be in the spotlight, but they are mostly Owls and Doves and probably wouldn't like it, including Dolores Woodington, Cathryn Plum, Chris Askew, Alex Woodington, and Olivia Villalon-Iglesias.

A huge thank you to Jeanne Eichler for your creativity and to Dr. Jeffrey Dayno for your valuable knowledge about the nervous system and the brain. Also, to Melissa Hess, I appreciate your Owl attention to detail.

To Kari Brownlie for designing a cover that reflects the essence of Personality Intelligence and Brian Kannard for turning this manuscript into a book. And a special thanks to Richard Ellis and Vanessa Ta. Your skillful way with words elevates my work.

Above all, my deepest gratitude goes to my wife, Traci, for her unwavering support and for keeping it real throughout this grand adventure.

Disclaimer

Any resemblance to actual people is purely intentional.

I mean, unintentional. Well, one of those.

Contents

Part III: The Four Styles and Personality Intelligence

Part IV: Increasing Your Personality Intelligence

Introduction

Since millions of people take personality assessments and attend training courses every year, we must be the most self-aware generation to have ever walked the Earth. I mean, how could we not be? Right now, you can find out which *Game of Thrones* or Disney character you are most like. The internet will tell you which car, city, or dog matches your personality. With all this self-awareness, we can't help but have perfect jobs, perfect relationships, and perfect lives, right? We should all be glowing in our awesomeness!

Not glowing yet? It's time to fix that.

Here's the issue: personality assessments and most corporate development programs based on them create fleeting fascination and, at best, help people reach an acceptable level of dysfunction. Rarely do these experiences unlock anyone's full potential.

Think about the process. Everyone gets identified as a specific type—I'm a C, he's Green, she's Fire, they're Sanguine, you're Daenerys Targaryen, and we're Elsas. Because no one can remember all the letters, colors, and random titles (except, perhaps, their own), they walk away focused on who they are, but not on who they could be.

My first two books, *Taking Flight!* and *The Chameleon*, tried to break this pattern (and don't worry, they're not prerequisites for reading *Personality Intelligence*). They introduced the four bird styles—Eagle, Parrot, Dove, and Owl—and the idea of adapting to different people and situations, the way a chameleon adapts to its surroundings became part of everyday life for many individuals and organizations. Still, it felt like there was a vast gap between learning the styles, mastering one's own style, and using them with Chameleon-like fluidity.

But what if an understanding of all the styles—not just our own—revealed the path to becoming the highest expression of ourselves? This book is a catalyst for that transformation.

You are about to learn how to harness the traits that make you uniquely you. On this journey, you will trace your style's growth from its early, undeveloped state to a typical level of function to style mastery. But it doesn't end there. You will learn to become the Chameleon, able to embody and leverage every style.

Along the way, you will likely take a hard look in the mirror. You will see yourself at your best and at your worst. You will notice how your style has fueled both your successes and hard lessons. Most intriguing, you might see a glimpse of the person you can become if you unlock the strengths of all the styles.

In short, Personality Intelligence is one's ability to understand the styles, recognize the styles in oneself and others, and tap into the full power of the styles. *Personality Intelligence* is your guide to becoming the Chameleon. It's time to transcend that personality assessment and training. Let the journey begin.

Part I:
The Four Styles

Chapter 1:
Eagles, Parrots, Doves, and Owls

For the first eighteen years of my career, I taught the DISC styles to people at companies around the world. The DISC model helps people understand their behavioral tendencies and how they interact with others, making it a valuable tool in the workplace—and beyond—for communication, teamwork, and leadership development. After leading a session, I would return six months later, and people would ask, "What is the D again?" "What does the S stand for?"

I felt like saying, "You're killing me! We spent an entire day on this!"

Therein lies the problem. You can't use the styles if you don't remember them.

Throughout history, there have been many four-style systems that describe personality types. In my system, they are represented by four birds. They're easy to remember, and their characteristics are universally recognized.

The Eagle is someone who is take-charge, direct, and confident. The Parrot is fun, enthusiastic, and talkative. Doves create a sense of harmony, caring, and consideration. Owls are factual and embody logic and precision. If the styles are intuitive today, they will be intuitive five years from now.

There is no deciphering step with the birds. In other systems, if someone's personality type is described as a letter or a color, you might need a moment to think, *D or red is dominant. That means that they are bottom-line and assertive. Therefore, I better get to the point quickly.* By then, you're already slow to get the point! And that's a lot of thinking needed to apply the styles.

While this book examines each style's traits and developmental path, none of us embodies just one style. You are a blend of all the styles to varying degrees, with one or two likely exerting more influence on your behavior. Your dominant style may occasionally lead you into trouble because you use it too much or too intensely, just as your least developed style can create problems if you don't access it when the situation calls for it.

To develop Personality Intelligence, we need a model to explain who we are, and we need a deep understanding of how styles appear in everyday life. So, let's get to it.

And hey, if you are very familiar with the Eagles, Parrots, Doves, and Owls and want to jump right to Chapter 3, go for it. I'll see you there.

The Four Styles and the Chameleon

In nature, there are approximately sixty species of eagles, four hundred varieties of parrots, three hundred types of doves, two hundred twenty species of owls, and two hundred chameleon species. Although all eagles share commonalities, each eagle species is distinct. Likewise, just because two individuals are Eagles, that doesn't mean they are the same; our life experiences and hardwiring shape our thoughts, feelings, and actions. Even identical twins who start with nearly identical DNA and grow up in the same house can be vastly different.

Let's meet the crew!

The Eagle

With their eight-foot wingspan, eagles float on thermal winds at ten thousand feet. They symbolize dominance, keen vision, and unwavering determination. Like their aviary counterparts, people with the Eagle style see opportunities from a distance. They focus on their goals and work diligently to achieve them.

Once eagles lock in on their target, they will not be deterred. If a young eagle picks up a salmon that is too heavy, it will sooner drown than let go of its quarry. Human Eagles are renowned for their relentless approach to challenges, too; they can be stubborn. They take risks and tackle obstacles head-on, demonstrating courage and resilience in the face of adversity.

In nature, eagles strategically plan their hunt and then dive at over one hundred miles per hour. Their human counterparts also think and act quickly in pursuit of their objectives. Eagles are known for their self-reliant, independent nature. They have confidence in *their* abilities but not necessarily in those of others. You don't see eagles flying in a V formation; they fly alone.

While anyone of any style can be a leader, Eagles revel in roles of authority. They focus on big-picture goals and help to remove obstacles to success. They talk straight and don't sugarcoat their words. Eagles are competitive and have the drive to win—they make things happen.

As the old axiom goes, "Too much of a good thing is not a good thing." The same is true with styles. When we overuse a strength, it becomes a weakness. When Eagles push their style needle into the Red Zone, their straight talk can become blunt and insensitive, hurting the feelings of those around them (especially the Doves). Their natural leadership abilities turn domineering, and their risk-taking becomes reckless. Their confidence grows into arrogance, which can become narcissism if dialed up too high.

The Parrot

If you come across a pandemonium of parrots—yes, a group of parrots is called a pandemonium—in the wild, you may need earplugs. Like their colorful and expressive counterparts, human Parrots are talkative and boisterous. They always have a story to tell.

Parrots have a knack for sharing their every thought and emotion with flair, making their communication style engaging and memorable. They enjoy interacting with just about anyone, familiar or not, so they tend to thrive in social settings. Their vibrant style makes them the life of the party; they draw others in with their charm.

Parrots have a zest for life and always find the bright side, even in the darkest moments. They are future-focused and believe that tomorrow will be sunnier than today. They often find ways to turn even the most daunting challenges into opportunities for growth and joy.

You will find that Parrots are playful and fun, spontaneous and unfazed. *Our plans were canceled? No worries. We'll make new ones, and they will be even better!*

These colorful individuals thrive in creative pursuits, where they can share out-of-the-box ideas that are crazy but just might work. They enjoy new experiences and have an appetite for the unusual and different.

When Parrots turn the style dial too high, they become ungrounded from reality. They may dismiss obvious dangers and impulsively take risks. Their ability to multitask degenerates into scattered chaos in which little is accomplished. Their formerly effective persuasive skills become manipulative.

The Dove

Doves are universal symbols of peace, love, and compassion. Like the graceful dove, individuals embodying this style bring a calming presence and a spirit of unity to their communities.

Doves often place the needs of those around them above their own well-being. If you've ever heard someone being asked for their preference between two things and respond, "I don't care, whatever makes you happy," you've likely witnessed a Dove in action. In nature, a dove will lure a predator away from the flock by pretending to be injured.

Doves genuinely care about others, offering support and understanding during difficult times. They are known for their intuitive ability to sense the unstated. Just as doves verbalize with a gentle cooing sound, those with the Dove style speak softly and kindly. They take care not to cause offense and may avoid expressing their desires directly for fear of upsetting others.

Conflict is uncomfortable for Doves, who strive to create harmony and balance. While they may hesitate to fight for themselves, the claws come out when you cross someone in their flock, such as a loved one or team member. They are highly protective of those that they care about.

Doves thrive in collaborative groups. When a dove finds food, they call the rest of the flock so they can eat as well. Those with the Dove style value unity and a sense of togetherness in their personal and professional endeavors. They do not like excluding anyone.

Dove loyalty and consistency extends to people, products, and rituals. It's Tuesday, which is Spaghetti Night. And when Doves discover they don't have spaghetti in the pantry, they get flustered. Let's not even talk about what happens if their favorite brand of toilet paper is out of stock.

Dialed too high, the Dove's overflowing abundance of love can smother those around them. Picture the grandmother who asks you if you want more food during your holiday dinner. After you say no, she puts more on your plate anyway and then packs even more neatly with ice packs for the drive home. Doves can become over-givers who ironically don't listen when others say they don't want assistance.

In the Red Zone, Doves passively wait for someone else to make decisions or take action. They can become conflict-avoidant and try hard to pretend that everything is fine.

The Owl

While owls are often associated with wisdom, it's important to note that anyone of any style can be smart. Nevertheless, nearly every cartoon owl is depicted as wise, and many wear glasses despite their incredible eyesight. What's the deal with that?

In many cultures, owls symbolize knowledge, introspection, and a keen sense of perception. Owls observe the world around them, patiently taking in the tiniest details.

Everything about the owl is sharp, from its razor-like talons to its laser-like night vision. Individuals with the Owl style share similar abilities to discern details that may elude everyone else. Their observational skills and attention to detail set them apart; if an Owl is going to do something, they are going to do it the right way.

You may not notice owls in the forest, as they blend seamlessly into the background. The shape of the owl's feathers allows it to fly silently. By one estimate, there is one owl within ten square miles of nearly every person in the United States. By contrast, if there were a Parrot within ten square miles of every person in the United States, we would know it!

People with the Owl style tend to be quiet and reserved, but make no mistake: you will hear from them if they believe that mistakes are about to be made. And if there is something they do not understand, brace yourself for a multitude of questions.

This stems from their need to think through things, though occasionally, it may seem like they're resistant to new ideas.

Known for their introspective nature, Owls engage in deep self-reflection. As such, they exude a calm and collected demeanor. They remain unruffled in the face of challenges, contributing to a sense of stability in their interactions.

Unlike Parrots, who enjoy social gatherings, Owls are often solitary. At work, they may prefer to do things themselves, in a private office or wearing a pair of noise-cancelling headphones. They could ask for help, but since their inner voice tells them that things will not be done correctly if delegated, they prefer to do things themselves.

When Owls crank the style dial high, they become perfectionistic. Their drive for accuracy can lead to analysis paralysis, making them critical of themselves and others.

Owls can get trapped in black-and-white—right or wrong—thinking. This inflexibility can create issues when emotions are involved. Pack the dishwasher incorrectly or take eggs randomly from the carton in the wrong order, and you may have to deal with the Owl in the Red Zone.

The Chameleon

In nature, chameleons are highly adaptable creatures. By changing the color of their skin to match their surroundings, they can blend into the landscape to avoid predators. They also use their color-changing ability to communicate with other chameleons. The colors can reflect an aggressive or dominant stance or their mood, health, and stress level. Chameleons thrive in various environments, from dense forests to arid deserts, making them remarkable survivors. They are the perfect symbol of adaptability.

The idea of the adaptable chameleon has ancient roots. Many cultures worldwide share tales of shapeshifters who represent themes of change and adaptability. The Navajo speak of Skinwalkers—sorcerers able to take on animal forms. Other notable examples include Loki from Norse legends, Proteus from Greek lore, Hanuman from Hindu epics, the Púca from Celtic stories, Leshy from Slavic tales, and the Nahuales in Aztec beliefs.

In terms of Personality Intelligence, the Chameleon represents the blend of all four styles. In a Venn diagram with four overlapping circles, each symbolizing the Eagle, Parrot, Dove, and Owl, at the intersection of these circles is the Chameleon.

The Chameleon does not represent a separate style but rather an individual's ability to shift between the four styles. The Chameleon is not bound by a single way of being but instead embodies what is called for in the moment.

Chameleons understand that different circumstances require different behaviors, whether it's the bold decisiveness of the Eagle, the enthusiastic positivity of the Parrot, the harmonious and supportive nature of the Dove, or the analytical precision of the Owl. By embodying elements of all these styles, the Chameleon can communicate effectively and thrive in any environment.

As you will soon discover, Chameleons represent the highest form of Personality Intelligence, as they care about what others need. Their adaptable nature enables them to connect with people from all walks of life.

Are People Just One Style?

Very few individuals exhibit just one style, except Spock in *Star Trek*. He is pretty much all Owl. But hey, he is half human and struggles with keeping his Dove side at bay. So, there's that.

Full-fledged humans use all four styles to varying degrees. Some have a primary style and a secondary style. Some even have a strong third style, called a tertiary style.

In a recent analysis of over one hundred thousand style-based assessments conducted by my organization, Take Flight Learning, we found that 7 percent of individuals had a strong primary style without a secondary style. This suggests their behavior largely flows from a single style. Meanwhile, 59 percent have both a primary and secondary style, meaning that two styles shape their actions. Another 33 percent added a third or tertiary style. A style is considered primary, secondary, or tertiary if it appears above the midline in the style graph. Styles above the midline tend to energize the individual, while those below it generally drain energy.

Chameleons aren't depicted by a flat graph at the midline that shows equal representation of all four styles. Instead, their profile typically highlights one, two, or three predominant styles, although they maintain the flexibility to seamlessly access all of them.

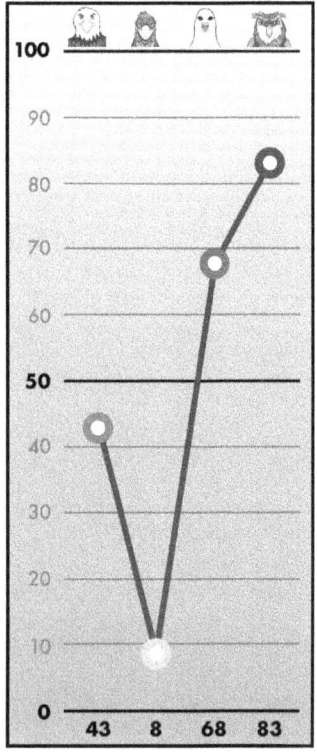

There is no doubt that people adapt their behaviors to their environment. You may act one way at work and another at home. And when the kids are absent, you may display different behaviors with your spouse than when they are present. You may behave differently in a meeting with your team members than with your manager. You may act one way at a family gathering and another when attending services at a house of worship. Learning how to shift your style to match the person or setting is a strength you will develop as you read this book.

Up Next

You don't need a degree in history or neuroscience to develop Personality Intelligence, but some awareness of where the styles come from and why there are four is helpful. The following chapter will explore how our brains shape our personality.

Chapter 2:
Mapping the Mind

Biology lays the foundation for our personalities, but it doesn't lock our identity in place. Our brains are remarkably adaptive—they can adjust to new stimuli and demands, allowing our personalities to evolve over time. This is referred to as neuroplasticity.

However, our neural wiring tends to favor authenticity, often resisting when we try to adopt behaviors that aren't true to our nature. This dynamic interplay between our biological makeup and our experiences means that we're continually growing and reshaping ourselves, proving that change is not only possible but a natural part of life.

It's often said that models are tools for the mind. So, let's journey back in time to explore the various frameworks that have sought to explain the essence of who we are.

A Brief History of Personality and the Four Styles

For millennia, people have grappled with the question of what makes us who we are. Despite being separated by vast spans of time, cultural differences, and great distances, philosophers and, later, psychologists consistently identified the same four core behavioral styles. How did these diverse thinkers arrive at the same model?

Let's start with the modern definition of *personality* and then we will work our way back. The American Psychological Association (APA) defines personality as "the individual differences in characteristic patterns of thinking, feeling, and behaving."

Notice that personality comprises not only our inner landscape of thoughts and emotions but also how we express ourselves through our actions and interactions. Our behavior, communication style, and the way we respond to different situations all serve as external reflections of who we are. This outward manifestation is just as critical as our internal experiences because it shapes how others perceive us and how we navigate the world. In essence, while our inner thoughts and feelings form the core of our personality, our actions provide a tangible expression of that core in everyday life.

"Personality" is a combination of two concepts: Type Theory, which has existed for over two thousand years, and Trait Theory, which emerged in the early 1900s.

Type Theory posits that personality types are a collection of traits—patterns of thought, emotion, or behavior that vary from person to person—that consistently occur together. A

"Healer" combines caring, helpfulness, selflessness, and patience. A "Warrior" is tenacious, daring, honorable, and results-driven. Notice how well a single word can capture a basket of traits.

Trait Theory measures specific characteristics or traits that make up an individual's personality. In this view, traits exist on a spectrum, meaning a person possesses each trait to a varying degree.

Let's use introversion and extroversion to understand the distinction between types and traits.

According to Type Theory, you are either an introvert or an extrovert. Steve Jobs was Apple's charismatic extrovert, while Steve Wozniak, the computer programming co-founder, was an introvert who focused on the technical aspects of their projects. On the television show *Friends*, Rachel is an extrovert, and Ross is an introvert. On *Modern Family*, we have Cam and Mitch. And on *The Simpsons*, Homer and Marge.

Trait Theory suggests that introversion and extroversion exist on a continuum. Imagine a bell-shaped curve where each person occupies a spot along the spectrum. Approximately 16% of the population falls in the introvert range, while another 16% falls in the extrovert range. The remaining 68% occupy the middle of the curve and are referred to as ambiverts, as they balance traits from both ends of the scale.

Most models based on types or styles have four distinct categories—not eight, not ten, not twenty, but exactly four. When we get to the neuroscience of the styles, we will explore why, but for now, let's head back to ancient Greece.

While types may have originated in Egypt or Mesopotamia, in 400 BC the Greek physician Hippocrates was seeking to describe the connection between physical health and emotional state. He developed the first typology based on four body fluids or "humours": Yellow Bile, Blood, Phlegm, and Black Bile. These four humours parallel the styles used today in the DISC model, leading one to wonder why we needed new terms when we could have easily referred to a person as primary Phlegm with secondary Yellow Bile. Go figure.

Around 160 AD, the Greco-Roman physician Galen built on Hippocrates' work with the first typology of temperaments: Choleric, Sanguine, Phlegmatic, and Melancholic. Meanwhile, about 5,000 miles away, the Chinese developed a system of their own. They created the Five Elements, known as the Wu Xing, which describe interactions and relationships between natural phenomena. Once the Five Elements came to maturity, sometime during the Han dynasty in the second or first century BC, it was adopted by thinkers in feng shui, astrology, medicine, military strategy, martial arts, and personality.

The Chinese Five Elements are Fire, Earth, Metal, Water, and Wood. You will notice that there are five elements, not four. In the Personality Intelligence system, the Earth and Water elements combine to form the Dove style. Earth represents the receptive, receiving, feminine yin aspect of the Dove—think Mother Earth—while water represents the active, giving, masculine yang aspect.

In North America, the Native American Medicine Wheel, also known as the Sacred Hoop, related the styles to the four directions, seasons, stages of life, and animals, such as the Wolf, Bear, Mouse, and Coyote. While different words represent the styles, they parallel the Greek and Chinese classifications.

Now let's fast forward to the 1900s; in 1928, Dr. William Moulton Marston introduced the DISC model in his book *The Emotions of Normal People*. He created a framework with four styles that divided behavior into two primary dimensions: perception of the environment, which he placed on the x-axis, and level of assertiveness or sense of power in the environment, on the y-axis. In the four-quadrant graph, on the left, people perceive the world as Antagonistic and hostile, and on the right, as Favorable and friendly.

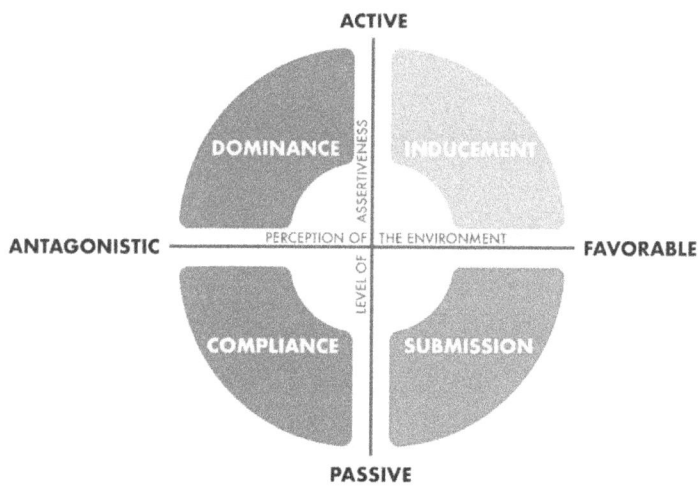

Those who perceive the world as Antagonistic see their environment as challenging, threatening, and filled with obstacles. They expect conflicts and difficulties in their interactions. They might say, "I don't trust people I don't know because they can let me down."

Those who perceive the world as Favorable believe that their environment is supportive, that people mean well, and that opportunities are available to those who look for them. They might say, "There is so much good in the world."

At the top of the graph, people who are Active perceive themselves as more powerful than their environment. They believe they can influence and control their environment, as they are self-assured in their ability to effect change and assert their will. "Put me in charge, and I'll make it happen," they might say.

On the bottom, Passive individuals believe they cannot control their environment. They tend to think they have limited influence to change the world. They might think, *I'm a small fish in a big ocean, at the mercy of powerful, external forces.*

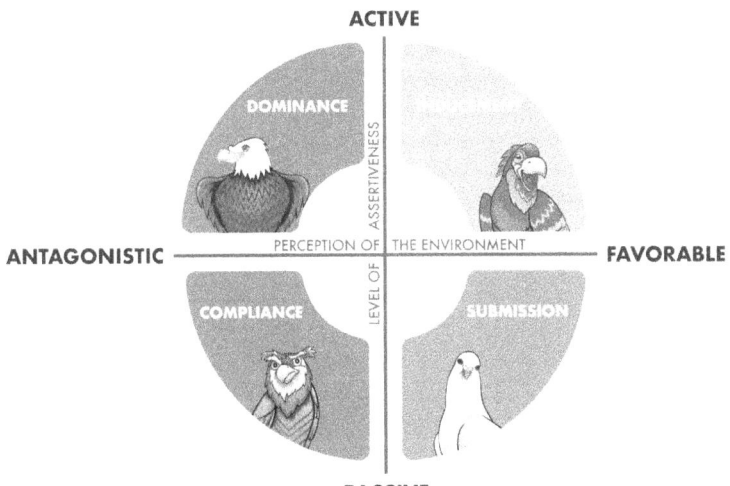

Eagles are in the top left quadrant and perceive the world as hostile. They also see themselves as having power over their world. Therefore, if they take control, they won't be taken advantage of and will be victorious. If they are in charge, they are safe.

Parrots, in the top right, also view themselves as more powerful than the environment but see the world as friendly. This is the root of their optimism. If you have the ability to create your reality and people are generally kind and helpful, why worry about anything? Things will always work out.

Doves, in the bottom right, also view the world as friendly, but they see themselves as less powerful than the environment. They find strength in the collective rather than the individual. Therefore, if they can align with the group and minimize conflict, they will be safe in an unfavorable environment.

Owls, located in the bottom left, see themselves as less powerful than their environment. But like Eagles, they perceive the world as Antagonistic; therefore, there is no room for criticism if they do everything perfectly. Plus, they believe they will be protected from danger if they follow the rules and ensure everyone else adheres to them as well. They can't control the world, but they can bring some order to the chaos by doing things the right way.

Marston's model explains how individuals trust themselves and others. For Parrots and Doves, since the world is friendly, trust is given without conditions. They open themselves up to vulnerability. However, if someone violates their trust, it creates a deep wound that won't heal easily.

Since, to Eagles and Owls, the world is dangerous, they don't allow themselves to be vulnerable. If someone breaks their trust, their worldview that people cannot be trusted until they have proven themselves to be trustworthy is reinforced.

While other models captured the four styles, Marston's DISC letters are likely the most widely used behavioral assessment in companies around the world—and have influenced my work.

Fun fact: Astute readers will notice that I pay homage to Marston's DISC model in the various fables and vignettes contained in this book as well as in my other books, *Taking Flight!*, *The Chameleon*, *Which Bird Are You?*, and *Flight School*. Later, you will meet **D**awn, **I**an, **S**carlett, and **C**arter.

Let's synthesize what we've learned so far. There are four styles. First up are the forthright, goal-oriented, and independent individuals. This would be Hippocrates's Yellow Bile humour, Galen's Choleric temperament, the Chinese element of Wood, and Marston's Dominance (D) in the DISC model. Along with the Native Americans, I call this the Eagle style.

Next are those who are sociable, charismatic, and animated. This would be Hippocrates's Blood humour, Galen's Sanguine temperament, the Chinese element of Fire, the Native American Coyote, and Marston's Inducement (I) style. These are the Parrots.

The friendly, helpful, soft-spoken Dove corresponds to Hippocrates' Phlegm humour, Galen's Phlegmatic temperament, and two Chinese elements: yin Earth and yang Water. Marston called this the Submissive (S) style, while the Native Americans named it the Buffalo.

Finally, Owls are precise, curious, and inquisitive. They are Black Bile according to Hippocrates and Melancholic in Galen's system. They are the Metal element in China and the Bear in the Native American's Sacred Hoop. Marston called them Compliant (C).

Hippocrates Humors 400 B.C.E.	Choleric	Sanguine	Phlegmatic	Melancholic
Aristotle Elements 350 B.C.E.	Air	Fire	Water	Earth
China Elements 200 B.C.E.	Wood	Fire	Earth/Water	Metal
Native Americans Medicine Wheel origin unknown	Eagle	Coyote	Buffalo	Bear
William Marston Behavioral Styles 1928	Dominance	Inducement	Submission	Compliance
Merrick Rosenberg *Taking Flight!* 2012				

The Neuroscience of Personality

The similarity of the four styles worldwide begs the question, *Why are there four types in each of these models?* Is it a cosmic coincidence that people from these disparate cultures separated by time and space identified the same four?

The answer is a resounding no and the reason lies within our brains. Neuroscientists have linked personality traits to brain structure and chemistry. So, put on your Owl hat and let's see how our brains create the four styles and reward us for being who we are.

We will start with the left and right sides of the brain. In the 1950s, neuroscientist Roger Sperry was awarded the Nobel Prize for his split-brain research. He realized that the left and right sides of the brain correspond to personality types. Left-brained people tend to be more quantitative, logical, and questioning. These are our task-focused Eagles and Owls. Right-brained, relationship-oriented Parrots and Doves are more intuitive, artistic, and carefree. Left-brained individuals create and stick to a financial plan or budget, while those who are right-brained spend it on good times and bonding experiences.

Also, in the 1950s, cardiologists Meyer Friedman and Ray Rosenman examined the predictors of heart disease. After a ten-year study, they were surprised to find that personality was a leading factor. This led to their creation of Type A and Type B Theory of Personalities.

Type A individuals are eager, highly competitive, and work hard to achieve goals. They can also be impatient and have poor judgment. For them, success is measured by quantity, not quality. These are Eagles and Parrots. They go on vacation and spend an hour on the beach, then declare, "Beach accomplished. Now what?"

By contrast, Type B people are easy-going and non-competitive, enjoy complex tasks, and seek accuracy. They are mild-mannered and don't feel the pressure of pressing deadlines. They seek quality over quantity. These are the Owl and Doves. Rather than getting frustrated in traffic, they listen to music or an audiobook, viewing the extra time as an opportunity to relax.

Friedman and Rosenman estimated that in healthy men between the ages of 35 and 59, those with the Type A personality had twice the risk of coronary heart disease compared to Type B people.

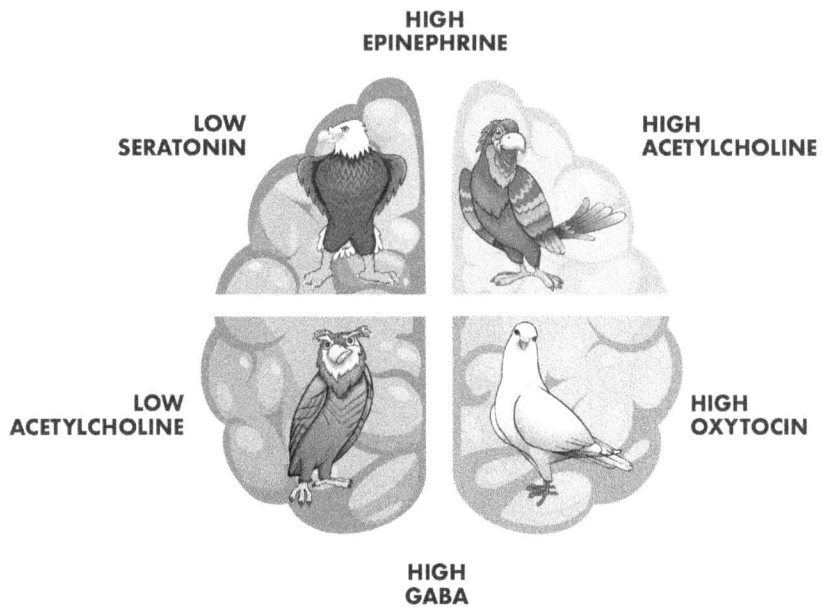

So, Type A people are the Active folks at the top of Marston's four quadrants, and Type B are the Passive folks at the bottom.

If we combine Type A and Type B with Left-Brained and Right-Brained, the brain mirrors the DISC model. Four quadrants, four styles.

Keep those Owl hats on for just a little while longer as we explore how brain chemistry and function also determine who we are.

The sympathetic nervous system, known as the "full-throttle" system, prepares us for "fight or flight." It switches on during the fast-paced, dynamic, high-intensity situations in which Eagles and Parrots thrive. However, in fight-or-flight mode, they may fail to recognize the consequences of their actions and may not adapt their plans when things go awry. There's no time to reflect and reconsider. These are the extroverts who are energized by action, interaction, and risk-taking.

Doves and Owls do much better when the parasympathetic nervous system, the "rest and digest" system, is operating. They tend to conserve energy and withdraw to their inner world of thoughts, feelings, memories, and ideas. This applies to introverts who appreciate an even-paced, patient way of doing things that leaves space and time to reflect on experiences calmly. However, in rest-and-digest mode, people tend not to take big risks or execute big plans. It's like that feeling you get after eating a big, rich meal— you're not going anywhere or doing anything too quickly.

Introverts and extroverts come in two varieties—task-oriented and people-oriented—which creates the four styles. Agentic, task-oriented extroverts are the Eagles. These go-getters have more gray matter in the medial orbitofrontal cortex, an area of the brain related to execution and reward. Affiliative, people-oriented extroverts are "people" people. They are the Parrots and have more gray matter in the medial orbitofrontal cortex, which is related to social cognition and behavior.

Task-oriented introverts are the Owls and have thicker gray matter in the prefrontal cortex, which links to logical thinking and decision-making. Social introverts, the Doves, have a highly active ventromedial prefrontal cortex, which is where empathy and emotions are processed.

If we went no further in linking the styles to the left and right brain, Type A and B, introversion and extroversion, and the

AGENTIC
EXTROVERTS

AFFILIATE
EXTROVERTS

THINKING
INTROVERTS

SOCIAL
INTROVERTS

sympathetic and parasympathetic nervous systems, we would understand why styles are consistent across time and geography.

But, tap into your inner Owl for a moment longer because we are going deeper. Recent discoveries in neuroscience have linked brain chemistry and hormones to personality. Individuals driven by the hormone epinephrine, also known as "adrenalin junkies," thrive in thrilling or dangerous situations. When they engage in dangerous activities, their brains flood with epinephrine, which energizes and encourages them to take more risks. These are your Eagles and Parrots.

Eagles tend to have low levels of the neurotransmitter serotonin, which neuroscientists have linked to higher levels of aggression and reduced impulse control. It helps explain why

Eagles act according to their own rules without considering how their behavior affects others. They can also be short-sighted and tend to assume that big risks come with big rewards, which isn't always true. Parrots, meanwhile, tend to have high levels of the neurotransmitter acetylcholine, which is linked to social behavior. No wonder Parrots are so group-oriented and talkative.

Moving to the bottom brain, Doves and Owls share high Gamma-Aminobutyric Acid (GABA) levels. People high in GABA tend to be more relaxed, demonstrate reduced stress levels, and appear calm and balanced.

It's no coincidence that Doves have high levels of oxytocin, also known as the "calm and cuddle" hormone. These folks are more trusting, generous, nurturing, approachable, and harmonious.

Unlike Parrots, Owls tend to have low levels of acetylcholine. This facilitates perfectionism, rigidity, difficulty making decisions, and decreased sociability.

So, there it is. Our styles are based on brain structure and the biochemistry that mediates brain function. Ancient philosophers couldn't scan and study the brain like we can, but they recognized these same patterns through observing people, which is remarkable!

The neuroscience of personality is essential to understand because our brain rewards us for being our authentic selves. When we display behaviors aligned with our personality, our brains follow the familiar pathways of existing hardwiring and release a satisfying dose of the neurotransmitters we crave. When a Dove offers care and support, they experience a surge of oxytocin, the "calm and cuddle" hormone. It's like the brain's way of saying, "Well done. Here's my way of thanking you."

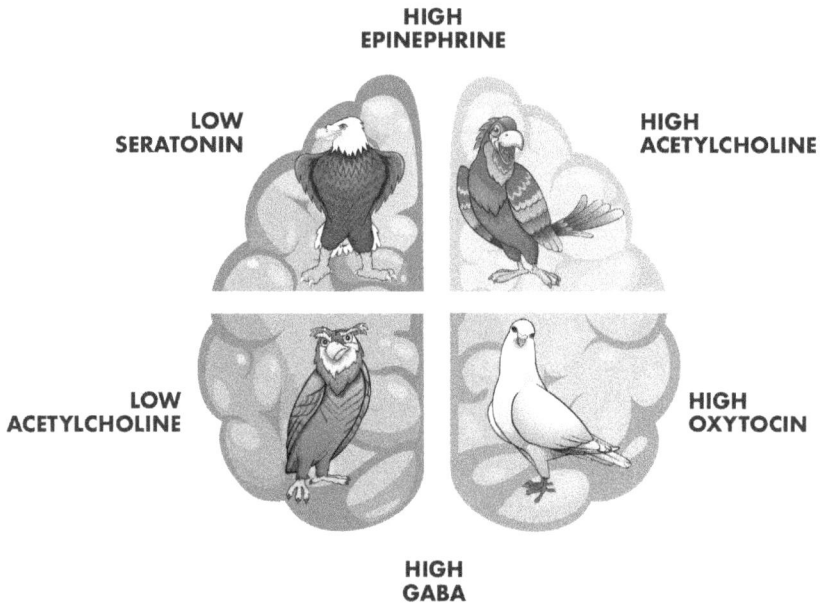

This built-in reward system also explains why stepping outside of our natural style may feel uncomfortable. However, with practice and intentionality, new neural pathways can form, making those behaviors easier to exhibit.

All of this underscores the importance of striving to be *our* best selves rather than what others or society want us to be. Our brains want us to be who we are!

Parrots, I see you. No more brain stuff. The following are the answers to two of the most commonly asked questions about the styles.

Does Style Change Over Time?

When I speak at conferences, the question I get asked most often is, "Does style change over time?"

Studies consistently reveal that personality stabilizes by the age of two or three. But don't our experiences and hard-fought wisdom change who we are?

Absolutely.

My experience working with hundreds of thousands of attendees at training programs and conferences suggests that style can indeed change. People regularly describe how much they've changed since childhood or even within a few years. In addition, neuroscientists have shown that the brain grows and changes in response to experiences.

That said, if someone is low in a particular style, it's less likely to develop into a dominant style and vice versa. For instance, a child who exhibits a strong Parrot style with minimal Dove is unlikely to grow into a robust Dove style with minimal Parrot traits.

Consider someone with a primary Owl and a secondary Eagle who studied finance and accounting in college. After she graduates and gets a job as an accountant, she likely spends the early years of her career in the weeds. Receipts. Invoices. Bills. Collections. You get the picture.

Advance twenty-five years, she is now the CFO at a five-hundred-person company. The organization's financial health depends more on her big-picture, strategic focus and less on her detailed, miss-nothing side. She monitors vital metrics such as revenue, profit margins, cash flow, budgets, and reports to shareholders. Over time, she transitions from being an Owl/Eagle to an Eagle/Owl.

By repeating new behaviors, we lay down new neural connections, and our style changes. Life experiences, personal relationships, careers, and significant events can all impact someone's style. Cultural influences, trauma, health changes, and life-altering epiphanies can also shape who we are.

So yes, style can change over time.

Do Styles Relate to Disorders?

Recall that William Marston introduced the DISC model in his book titled *The Emotions of Normal People.* In other words, the styles apply to "normal" people. Of course, we wouldn't use that word today, but I believe *normal* meant people with strengths and challenges. Let's face it: we are all a little dysfunctional, some more than others, but we get by. And the styles apply to all of us.

At extremes, however, the styles give way to disorders. Anyone of any style can have any disorder. However, certain disorders tend to correlate with particular styles.

Crank up the Eagle dial and confidence becomes arrogance. Turn it up even more and that turns into narcissism. Keep going and it becomes Narcissistic Personality Disorder. One more crank of the dial and there is Malignant Narcissistic Personality Disorder. Now, that's a scary place to visit. Brace for impact if that individual is your parent or boss.

At extreme levels, people transcend "normality," and the styles work against them. Eagles can gain an inflated sense of self-importance and an excessive craving for respect and control, that can lead them to exploit or belittle others to achieve their goals.

They can climb the corporate ladder by stepping on those beneath them and show little regard for other individuals.

When Parrots have an overwhelming craving to be liked and celebrated, they can reach the level of Histrionic Personality Disorder. At this level, Parrots seek to obtain the spotlight and be revered by all. They try to attract attention by exaggerating their stories and abilities and by being overly animated and dramatic. At this level, Parrots have an insatiable need to capture the spotlight and receive almost constant admiration and praise.

Turning up the dial on the Dove's thirst for harmony and acceptance can lead to Borderline Personality Disorder. These Doves fear conflict and have an unquenchable thirst for approval. As a result, they may become overly dependent, relying on others to make decisions for them and take responsibility for critical aspects of their life.

At an extreme level, the Owl's need for accuracy and consistency becomes Obsessive-Compulsive Personality Disorder. Extreme perfectionism and order create an overwhelming compulsion to impose their high standards and processes on the people in their life, which, ironically, often results in inefficiency and an inability to complete tasks.

When someone with the Eagle/Parrot combo style pushes the style dial too high, they may be prone to Oppositional Defiant Disorder. Their elevated level of confidence and self-efficacy may lead them to resist authority or push back hard against control, especially if they are young and lack self-regulation.

NARCISSISTIC
PERSONALITY
DISORDER

HISTRIONIC
PERSONALITY
DISORDER

OBSESSIVE
COMPULSIVE
PERSONALITY
DISORDER

BODERLINE
PERSONALITY
DISORDER

Owls and Doves have a rich inner world. If they get caught up in the negative aspects of that world, they can be prone to depression. While anyone can get depressed, these styles tend to internalize their feelings, and therefore, can lose themselves in their emotions.

To be clear, people at a very high level of their style don't necessarily have disorders. Richard Branson, founder of the Virgin Group, for example, likely has a very strong Parrot style. His enthusiasm, optimism, and extreme risk-taking have contributed to his immense success. It also nearly killed him in several hot-air balloon crashes. But that doesn't mean Branson has a disorder. It just means that he has an extraordinarily strong Parrot style.

Let's explore the various disorders through the characters in *Winnie the Pooh*. Tigger, who is bouncey, trouncey, ouncey, pouncey, fun, fun, fun, fun, fun, is the impulsive Parrot. He has difficulty sitting still or focusing on a single task, which makes him a likely candidate for Attention Deficit Hyperactivity Disorder (ADHD). This is the Parrot style at the disorder level.

As the antithesis of Tigger's zeal and positivity, Eeyore's pessimism and lack of energy would lead one to believe that he has dialed up his Owl or Dove style to the point of Major Depressive Disorder.

In an ironic twist, the Owl in *Winnie the Pooh* is an Eagle. He shows signs of self-importance and the urge to be seen as wise, which may indicate a bit of Narcissistic Personality Disorder.

Kanga, the Dove, is overprotective of her child, Roo. Her fear of social interaction and its implications may be indicative of Social Anxiety Disorder. Piglet, another Dove, is frequently anxious about potential danger, which Generalized Anxiety Disorder can cause.

Rabbit's Owl style, taken to a place of perfectionism and anxiety when things are out of order, might be a function of Obsessive-Compulsive Disorder (OCD).

Winnie the Pooh is the Dove/Parrot with a kind warmth and good appetite for social interaction (and honey). While there might be an unchecked eating disorder or honey addiction, Pooh's style is in a healthy zone. As for Christopher Robin, he thinks his imaginary friends are real—or maybe that his real friends are imaginary. Either way, something is going on there.

In all seriousness, when embodied at an extreme, the styles can become disorders. At that point, it is best to consult a mental health professional.

Up Next

Personality is deeply rooted in our genetics, brain chemistry, and lived experience. That explains why styles are surprisingly consistent across place and time. While some cultures might reward or praise traits associated with one style versus another, you'll find Eagles, Parrots, Doves, and Owls everywhere you go. In the next chapter, we'll delve into Personality Intelligence.

Part II:
Personality Intelligence

Chapter 3:
What Is Personality Intelligence?

Now that you're familiar with the four styles, we are ready to dive into Personality Intelligence.

Personality represents how we think, feel, and act. *Intelligence* is the capacity for understanding, learning, and reasoning. Together, they are defined as follows:

> Per·son·al·i·ty In·tel·li·gence
>
> /pərsnˈalədē Inˈteləj(ə)ns/ *noun*
>
> The ability to understand the Eagle, Parrot, Dove, and Owl styles, effectively leverage one's traits, recognize and interpret the styles of others, and authentically apply this knowledge to build healthy relationships and maximize potential.

Personality Intelligence is denoted as "PIQ," with "P" symbolizing Personality and "IQ" paying homage to the Intelligence Quotient.

Recall that styles represent a collection of traits. At times, we may be influenced by more than one style. The thoughts and feelings that influence the behaviors of our unique blend of styles shape our personality—and, ultimately, our Personality Intelligence.

The Components of Personality Intelligence

Personality Intelligence goes beyond recognizing how traits combine to form behavioral patterns. It's more than being aware of how these patterns show up. Personality Intelligence relies on several core aspects:

1. *Understanding the Eagle, Parrot, Dove, and Owl Styles*

    Although known by different names, the four have persisted for millennia for a reason—they distill the complexity of human behavior into an accessible, memorable model that explains why humans think and act as they do. People who understand the styles can use this knowledge as a building block for developing Personality Intelligence.

    While a small number of exceptional individuals develop Personality Intelligence naturally and without formal knowledge of the styles, most of us need a practical mental framework to get there.

2. *Recognizing the Pattern of One's Traits*

Individuals who understand their style are keenly aware of how they think, feel, and behave in various situations. They can anticipate their reactions, identify what energizes or drains them, draw on their style skills, and recognize areas for improvement. This self-awareness enables them to tackle challenges with intention.

3. *Leveraging the Styles to Be One's Best Self*

When someone masters their style, they can leverage their abilities to the fullest, free from the challenges of their natural traits. They integrate their style into every facet of their lives, using it to drive their growth, success, and happiness. This mastery enables them to navigate obstacles and turn them into opportunities.

4. *Reading the Styles of Others*

Quickly identifying someone's style enables individuals to adapt responsively to present and future scenarios. For instance, if you recognize that a spouse or customer is an Owl, you can anticipate their thirst for detailed information and their tendency to ask numerous questions if certain information is not provided. This understanding allows you to create a more positive interaction.

Master people-readers pick up on subtle cues in anyone's words, tone, rate of speech, facial expressions, and body language. In a split second, they can identify, *This person is an Eagle*, or *That person is a Dove/Parrot*. Being able to recognize the styles lays the foundation for supporting them.

5. *Capitalizing on All Four Styles to Achieve Full Potential and Build Healthy Relationships*

The final aspect of Personality Intelligence is to embody all four styles at the highest level. In this Chameleon state, individuals fluidly adapt to others without losing their authentic selves.

In so doing, Chameleons can interact successfully with anyone. They make people feel at ease and supported, treating them as *they* need to be treated instead of imposing their own style on others. They make a difference in the world just by being themselves. As parents, leaders, and teachers, they help others advance on their path to success. They don't revel in their own gifts but instead help others reveal theirs.

Personality Intelligence at Home

Nowhere is Personality Intelligence more important than with family, the people closest to us. Anyone who had a parent who did not accept them and tried to change them into someone else understands this deeply. As parents, the goal is to help our children be the best version of themselves, not the best version of us. Imagine an Eagle mother pushing her Dove son to be more aggressive and stop being sensitive. The unspoken message to her son is, *You are not okay the way you are, and I would love you if you were someone else—someone more like me.*

Anyone who has a brother or sister whose style varies greatly from their own likely has stories as well. There may have been a sibling who always seemed to find mischief and another who strictly adhered to the rules. Perhaps you had a brother or sister who acted like the boss of the entire family, and another who happily followed along. Looking back, you may find yourself saying, "Now I understand why" as you read this book.

We also see this in marriages, when people appear to marry someone for who they are, only to try to change them into who they want them to be after exchanging vows. Good luck with that! Individuals with highly developed Personality Intelligence accept others for who they are without judgment or the urge to change them. If you're looking for a reason to boost your Personality Intelligence, look no further than the ability to develop a healthier home life.

Personality Intelligence at Work

Given that we spend roughly a quarter of our waking lives at work, our Personality Intelligence has a massive impact on our career success. Imagine a Parrot manager who appreciates receiving upbeat, positive feedback. It's only natural for her to assume that others value the same type of feedback. One day, one of her Owl associates knocks a project out of the park. So, the Parrot manager walks down the hall, steps into the Owl's doorway, and, bursting with excitement, regales him with how amazing he is. "Incredible work! You totally rock. I couldn't have asked for anything more."

The manager leaves with the pride of being a motivational leader. Meanwhile, the Owl shakes his head and thinks, *What the heck was that? Anyway, back to work.*

Later that year, the Owl team member leaves the organization and, in his exit interview, reveals that he didn't feel like his work was valued. *How can that be?*, the Parrot manager wonders. *I can identify specific instances when I gave him feedback. I specifically remember a day when I went to his office and told him what a great job he did.*

The Owl doesn't recall it because the feedback lacked Personality Intelligence. The manager gave feedback in *her* style, not the recipient's style. Parrots provide upbeat and energetic feedback but lack the details that Owls crave. If she had approached him with Owl specifics about what she liked and suggestions for improvement, you can bet that the Owl would have felt appreciated. That's Personality Intelligence in action.

Now, let's meet Isaac, Scarlett, and her pet Cookie and see how Personality Intelligence plays out at home and work.

The Gerbil

Cookie was a feisty little gerbil. At three years old, he was in the sunset of his life. And what a life, as far as gerbil lives go. He had a loving family and a great place to live.

As far as five-year-old Scarlett was concerned, Cookie had always been there. Scurrying. Building. Sleeping. Moving this cereal box over here. Digging in the bedding over there. Scarlett enjoyed sharing Cookie with her friends. They spent endless hours watching and laughing at his silly antics.

But this was a school night, and first grade was serious. In his softest fatherly voice, Isaac told his daughter to get to bed. Scarlett approached her furry friend as she had done every night since Cookie entered her life, wishing him sweet dreams and whispering, "I love you, Cookie."

The following morning, Isaac was lying in bed, his alarm about to go off, when he felt someone watching him. His eyes shot open. Scarlett was standing beside him with tears in her eyes. In a quiet, shaky voice she said, "I tried to wake Cookie, but he won't get up."

Isaac had known this day would come but had hoped it wouldn't be so soon. And why today? He had so much to accomplish, and now he had to deal with Scarlett and Cookie. He felt the weight of what his daughter was about to go through. Scarlett's pain was palpable as he rattled the cage to no avail. This was the day. Cookie had passed in the night.

Isaac took his daughter's hand and walked her into the family room. He thought about how she hadn't yet known loss and how upset she was going to be.

Scarlett's eyes filled with tears as she asked, "Is he going to be okay?"

Isaac gathered her close as he explained that Cookie had passed away. He told her that he had gone to a better place, a place filled with toys and lots of other gerbils. He described how Cookie would play with new friends all day long.

Scarlett burst into tears. "But I was his friend. And he had lots of toys. Why did he leave? I thought he liked it here."

At that moment, Isaac realized that his first attempt at consoling Scarlett had been entirely off base. He took a breath and tried again. He spoke tenderly of the joy Cookie brought to their home. They shared stories of the love Cookie brought to their lives and the special memories they would always cherish. Scarlett's eyes reflected a mix of sadness and understanding as her dad reassured her that Cookie would forever hold a place in their hearts.

Isaac worked with Scarlett to create a farewell card adorned with drawings of Cookie and their favorite activities. Then he led a small ceremony in the backyard beneath a weeping willow tree as they talked about Cookie. Through shared tears and comforting hugs, Scarlett learned about love and loss as she said goodbye to her old friend.

Before dropping Scarlett off at school, Isaac wrote a note to her teacher explaining the morning's events and requesting compassion for his grieving daughter. On his way to work, Isaac felt the full weight of his little girl's sadness.

When he arrived at the office parking lot, he pulled himself together, dried his eyes, and steadied himself for his day. He went to the office kitchen and poured himself a cup of coffee. He took a sip as Dana, one of his coworkers, arrived for the second cup of her morning brew. She made a beeline for the coffee, as she was all business. Dana noticed Isaac's red eyes, and it didn't take long for her to realize he was upset. "What's wrong?" she asked.

Like a faucet, Isaac let the story of his morning come pouring out. He told her about Cookie and his daughter, their makeshift memorial, and the card emblazoned with the words, *To my best friend. You were the best gerbil ever.*

Despite feeling like this was a lot of emotion for a little gerbil, Dana stood up straight. Of all the problems she encountered every day, this one was fixable. She looked into her coworker's eyes and said, "Gerbils cost ten dollars. Just get another one." She was proud that she could offer a viable solution. She had offered a concrete way to make both Isaac and Scarlett feel better. Dana felt pretty good about herself, so Isaac's puzzled look utterly baffled her.

He huffed, rolled his eyes, and stormed out of the kitchen. *How could she be so insensitive,* he thought.

With black coffee in hand, Dana considered, *Come to think of it, it's too bad his daughter found the gerbil. He could have just swapped it for a new one, and she would have been none the wiser. My kids are on version three of our goldfish. Well, it's time to solve other problems. The day is early, and I'm already one-for-one.*

Isaac sat at his desk as Dana's words echoed in the background, "Just go get another one." He shook his head in disbelief. *You can't replace someone you love. It doesn't work like that.*

Throughout the day, Isaac tried to focus on his work, but Dana's advice kept interrupting his thoughts. She could have said, "I'm sorry for your loss," or "It sounds like you're having a hard day." Either of those would have been sufficient. How about a little compassion? Maybe, "I've lost pets, too" or "That's so sad." But *gerbils cost ten dollars, just replace him*? So insensitive! Isaac got angrier as the day wore on.

When he arrived home, Scarlett looked better than when he had left her that morning. It seemed she was bouncing back.

After putting her down for the night, Isaac sat with a cup of chamomile tea and wished he had told Dana how insensitive she was.

He took another sip and thought, *Maybe I* should *get Scarlett another gerbil.*

Reflections on "The Gerbil"

Let's practice one of the skills of Personality Intelligence: people-reading. Given Scarlett's relationship with Cookie and her response to his passing, it's reasonable to conclude she is a Dove. The way in which Isaac initially attempted to comfort Scarlett by trying to spin a sad situation into a positive one is a telltale sign that he is a Parrot. When Dana instantly shifted into problem-solving mode, despite Isaac's need for emotional validation, she exemplified Eagle energy.

At the outset, we see the Dove in action as we observe Scarlett interacting with her beloved gerbil. As for Isaac, he reflexively imposed his Parrot style on his daughter by trying to make everything seem okay. People with lower levels of Personality Intelligence often impose their style on others. However, notice how he pivoted quickly to match Scarlett's Dove style, demonstrating the awareness that he had to flex his style to meet his daughter's needs. His empathetic response gave her the space to grieve. This reveals that Isaac has progressed on his Personality Intelligence journey.

Conversely, Dana lacked the style-awareness to fully understand her own style and how it affects those around her. She was unable to assess what Isaac needed in their interaction, which is a crucial aspect of Personality Intelligence. While Isaac may be a Parrot, he was in Dove mode in his encounter with Dana, and she missed the opportunity to connect with him by responding in a Dove manner. This highlights the importance of not only understanding one's own style but also being attuned to what is needed in a specific interaction.

Treating others how *they* need to be treated, not how *we* want to be treated, is what I call the Home Rule. We help others feel at home by satisfying their style-driven preferences. Chameleons are adept at applying the Home Rule in every situation. Dana hasn't gotten there yet.

Up Next

Many more stories illustrating the power of style awareness, people-reading, and adaptability are to come. For now, it's time to explore the four levels, from the Unevolved State in the shadow to the fully illuminated Chameleon State.

Chapter 4:
The Four Levels of Personality Intelligence

Introducing the Four Levels

At this point, you know that the styles influence how we interact and handle challenges. Each style has unique talents and areas for growth. Sometimes, we feel stable and in control, allowing our style to shine. Other times, we may feel more anxious and reactive, displaying the shadow side of our style, where our strengths are less visible or underdeveloped. Ideally, we have more positive moments than difficult ones. Without an intentional approach to growth, a person's natural traits can limit their potential.

What if we view the styles as flexible and evolving rather than fixed? Instead of merely accepting that each style has limitations, what if we could tap into our style's innate wisdom and grow beyond its natural tendencies to reach a higher level of effectiveness?

As we place the styles on a growth continuum, individuals begin in the undeveloped state. At this initial stage, style weaknesses are

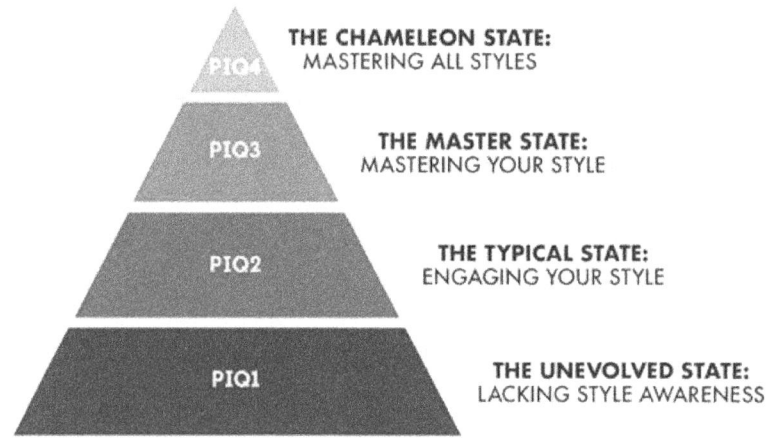

THE CHAMELEON STATE: MASTERING ALL STYLES

PIQ4

THE MASTER STATE: MASTERING YOUR STYLE

PIQ3

THE TYPICAL STATE: ENGAGING YOUR STYLE

PIQ2

THE UNEVOLVED STATE: LACKING STYLE AWARENESS

PIQ1

on full display. As individuals grow, they progress to a typical state, where their innate skills are expressed alongside their challenges. From there, they learn to express the highest version of their style and, ultimately, all the styles.

Before going into the levels in more detail, let's introduce some terminology that will be used throughout this book. For simplicity, Level 1 of Personality Intelligence will be referred to as PIQ1, Level 2 as PIQ2, Level 3 as PIQ3, and Level 4 as PIQ4.

The path begins with Level 1 of Personality Intelligence or PIQ1, where individuals are unevolved and have little understanding of their style and how it influences their behaviors and outcomes. This is where we begin as children, though adults can get stuck here. PIQ1 individuals experience self-limiting thoughts and exhibit behaviors that do not serve their best interests. While they may achieve success in some areas of life, they'll struggle to create healthy and enduring relationships.

As individuals grow, they move into Level 2 or PIQ2, where they begin to recognize and employ their natural gifts. Although they occasionally fall into the shadow aspects of their style, their strengths are developed enough that they lead happy and productive lives. The overwhelming majority of the population operates at this level. It's the stage in which we accept that weaknesses are a part of the human condition and is exemplified by phrases like, "We're not perfect" and "I'm only human."

At Level 3 or PIQ3, people soar. Having mastered their style, they take flight and attain a level of success that few ever achieve. These individuals transcend style-related issues. Negative thoughts are fleeting, and harmful behaviors—toward themselves or others—are minimal. When we meet people at this stage, we are drawn to them. They seem to have everything figured out.

Level 4, also known as PIQ4, is rare—*very* rare. These individuals master not only their own style but all the styles. These Chameleons possess extraordinary Personality Intelligence, making them highly effective leaders, collaborators, influencers, teachers, friends, and companions. They build deep bonds with people of all styles and walks of life, leaving a lasting impact wherever they go.

A Deeper Dive into the Four Levels

Now that you have a basic understanding of the four levels of Personality Intelligence, let's explore them further.

Level 1: The Unevolved State—
Lacking Style Awareness (PIQ1)

At this initial level, a person's style is just beginning to form. Most individuals at this stage lack the life experience to develop a strong sense of their style and don't know how to leverage their abilities. They haven't yet learned to manage their stress responses or regulate their behaviors effectively. As a result, their words and actions can sometimes lead to challenges at school, at work, or at home with family.

In the Unevolved State, individuals lack the flexibility to adapt and are confined to their style. They are typically driven by fear, though the nature of that fear varies by style. At Level 1, people rationalize their behavior when it causes harm to others. A PIQ1 Eagle might share unfiltered thoughts that hurt someone's feelings, then say, "I call it like it is."

Although the behaviors at this level can come across as selfish or disrespectful, they often reflect unmet needs and underlying fears. They are typically driven by internal struggles, such as insecurity or a craving for control, rather than a conscious intention to harm or disrespect others. The PIQ1 individual's actions arise from the drive to protect themselves or gain validation.

Level 1 people regularly overuse their strengths and push them into the Red Zone. Rather than simply being generous, a Dove is smothering. The Parrot's ability to multitask becomes scattered and disorganized. The Owl's obsession with perfection can cause them to spend hours on projects that could have taken twenty minutes. And the Eagle's confidence devolves into arrogance.

You'll notice that people go out of their way to avoid triggering friends, family, and coworkers who are at PIQ1. The road ahead is long for people at this Unevolved State.

Level 2: The Typical State— Engaging Your Style (PIQ2)

As individuals progress on their journey, they become more conscious and deliberate in their actions. Having experienced the consequences of their ineffective Level 1 patterns, they begin to replace old habits with more constructive ways of acting and interacting.

People at this stage have a core set of capabilities that help them in every aspect of life. Their style has likely drawn them to a career that allows their innate gifts to shine.

PIQ2 individuals have occasional moments of brilliance that are energizing and occasional times of regret in which they wish they had acted differently. Their ineffectual behaviors are typically caused by stress, which can drag them back to the Level 1 version of themselves. When the stressor fades, their abilities reappear.

At this stage, Eagles tend to assess situations quickly and take decisive action. However, they occasionally may act impulsively without fully considering the consequences. Parrots are likely to focus on the positive and may occasionally overlook looming problems. Doves will tend to offer stability and dependability, yet they can become entrenched in familiar routines and resist change. Owls likely bring deep focus and dedication to their work, but they may become so absorbed in the task that they lose touch with those around them.

At this Typical State of development, people accept the human condition as flawed. They understand that weaknesses will rear their ugly head every so often, and that's to be expected. As long as the good outweighs the bad, they are equipped to navigate life's challenges.

Level 3: The Master State— Mastering Your Style (PIQ3)

Level 3 is the highest stage of development within one's style. At this point, individuals have progressed from the lowest version of themselves to the Typical State to the best version of their style.

PIQ3 individuals masterfully balance the polarities of their style, demonstrating an acute awareness of how to leverage their innate skills while tapping into complementary abilities. By integrating these contrasting qualities, they gain a more holistic approach to problem-solving and interpersonal relationships, enhancing their effectiveness in diverse settings.

For instance, Level 3 Eagles temper their natural assertiveness with patience. They diligently pursue goals but also take time to listen to team members' ideas and feedback.

Parrots at this level channel their infectious energy into motivating others while balancing their positive vision for the future with a sober dose of reality. They can uplift the team with their passion but remain practical and acknowledge potential obstacles.

The master Dove shows abundant compassion while establishing healthy boundaries. They offer support and encouragement while being mindful of their limits, which they communicate clearly.

Level 3 Owls skillfully combine their analytical prowess with intuitive insights. While they excel at gathering and evaluating data to make informed decisions, they also rely on their instincts to avoid getting stuck in analysis paralysis.

At this level, individuals make full use of their style's abilities. A PIQ3 person's style may seem like the secret ingredient that fuels their success.

Level 4: The Chameleon State— Mastering All Styles (PIQ4)

If Level 3 is the ultimate stage of development within one's style, Level 4 is the penultimate expression of all four styles. This is the Chameleon State, in which individuals exhibit the highest level of flexibility by fluidly adapting to the right style for each situation.

PIQ4 individuals intuitively access the strengths and advantages of the Eagle, Parrot, Dove, and Owl. Regardless of their natural style, a strong Eagle at this level can effortlessly display compassion, and a full-on Parrot can digest and logically analyze a dense spreadsheet. The Dove comfortably takes charge while the Owl enthusiastically shares their exciting vision.

And yet, with the full range of responses in their repertoire, they express themselves with full authenticity. This ability to draw upon various styles allows them to communicate more effectively and supports strong, lasting relationships.

Those at Level 4 make people better by being present. Their actions create an uplifting ripple effect. They shine their style like a lighthouse, guiding others to safety, authenticity, and the yearning to be better.

When people reach the Chameleon State, they are no longer motivated by fear, but rather by love and acceptance of others. They act from a place of style awareness where they perceive themselves accurately with minimal self-deception. They have strong self-esteem, yet they are humble. They accept themselves for who they are and do not feel the need to conform to what society says they should do or be.

At Level 4, individuals have maximized their human potential.

Up Next

With a familiarity of the four levels of Personality Intelligence under your belt, it's time to explore how each of the styles is displayed at each level.

Chapter 5:
Personality Intelligence Level 1

Individuals move through distinct levels of understanding and applying their personality style just as martial artists progress through different ranks and skills. Each level, or rank, represents a stage of growth, mastery, and adaptability, allowing one to navigate interactions and challenges with increasing poise.

By drawing parallels to martial arts, we can better understand how each level enhances our ability to strengthen interpersonal ties, balance innate traits, and develop a deeper awareness of ourselves and those around us.

The Way of the Styles

In my freshman year of college, I joined a karate class. In that first class, I met a fellow student who would eventually become my wife. After we graduated, we opened a karate school and ran it together for over twenty-five years. There were no tournaments or trophies—the reward was becoming a better human.

Most new students entered our dojo, the place where martial arts are practiced, without any prior experience. When they put on their gi, or karate uniform, for the first time, they had pre-existing self-defense instincts. If someone tried to punch them in the face, they'd freeze, duck, or try to block the punch. Usually, their instinctive reaction didn't work, and the punch would land.

At the white belt level, students repetitively practice blocks to defend against punches and kicks. They repeat the blocking patterns tens of thousands of times. One block may protect the head, another the midsection, and a third the lower part of the body.

Early on, these techniques are remarkably ineffective. Getting into the proper position and performing the correct movement requires conscious thought, which slows the movement. New martial artists find it hard to maintain balance and release muscle tension, which inhibits speed and power. Everyone has instincts and martial arts blocking techniques are not part of them.

This stage parallels PIQ1, the Unevolved State of Personality Intelligence, where natural reactions may work against us. Sometimes, we get metaphorically whacked in the face in our jobs or in our relationships. We try our best, but it just doesn't work. Ultimately, we discover new behaviors and try them out to see if they get better results.

With time and practice, new techniques become hardwired in the martial artist. They can block without thinking about it first. Just as a new driver needs total focus the first time they get behind the wheel but requires less focus the more they drive. Years later, they can play harmonica while driving. Okay, maybe that's just me, but you get the point.

It takes about five to eight years of practicing martial arts to replace natural reactions with trained techniques. But once a technique is internalized, it becomes an instinct and kicks in (no pun intended) with little thought. This is when martial artists earn their black belt and are ready to learn karate for the first time. Yes, you heard me right—the black belt is the beginning rather than the end of learning a martial art. In a sense, the black belt is a beginner once more, having come full circle from white belt, through the colored belts, to the absence of color.

Picture a clock with "12" at the top, representing both noon and midnight. In martial arts, white and black belts both reside at "12." When the white belt takes their first class, they are at the top of the circle. Over time, through years of practice and hard work, they travel around the circle, earning colored belts until they return to the top, where they earn their black belt.

The rank of black belt in karate is colloquially called "cutting the cloth." This process, known in Japanese as koromogae, metaphorically means cutting away the old, like a tailor trimming a piece of cloth to make a new garment. In the martial arts, it signifies the shedding of the novice status and the beginning of a new journey as a black belt karateka, karate practitioner.

When an instructor ties the black belt around a student's waist for the first time, it's as if they are giving them a new gi to wear. Up to this point, the student had to wear their gi precisely as it was given; they couldn't change the gi in any way. Now, as a black belt, they can cut the cloth to alter the gi to fit them. They can adjust the techniques to suit their body and their personality. At this point, they must relearn every technique. The time has come to make the martial arts their own.

This cutting of the cloth happens between Level 1 and Level 2 of Personality Intelligence. Individuals are no longer operating on autopilot, exhibiting ineffective behaviors. Instead, with their new self-knowledge, they act with intention, using their style deliberately.

With those new instincts, they are far better equipped to handle whatever is thrown at them. Sometimes, they lose the match, but they put up a good fight. Their style helps them succeed, though it occasionally works against them.

Fast forward about five years, and the karate student travels around the circle again to become a second-degree black belt. It's like becoming a black belt for the first time, as they have learned the martial arts built on karate instincts instead of natural instincts. With each successive trip around the circle, they gain deeper knowledge and display their skills at a higher level.

As a fifth-degree black belt, I have theoretically circumnavigated the path five times, each time learning the martial arts with new eyes and a new foundation.

After many trips around the circle, a martial artist may ultimately attain mastery, though a true master believes there is always more to learn. Welcome to Level 3 of Personality

Intelligence, where individuals master their techniques and make them their own.

But the road does not end there. At Level 4, the grandmaster can take on any opponent at any level in any setting. Let's head into the dojo and watch Level 1 in action.

The Way of the Birds

Sensei Tori arrived early at his dojo, as he had done before every class for over forty years. It was the beginning of a new year, and he was eager to welcome four new students as they began their martial arts journey.

Sensei dutifully retrieved the broom from its place in the closet. He gracefully swept the studio floor with movements reminiscent of his martial arts training. His actions were fluid and controlled like a karate technique. He executed each movement with focused intention.

Dawn Eagleton walked through the door as Sensei made his final pass on the worn hardwood. Catching Dawn's gaze, Sensei gave a slight nod to his new student. Eight-year-old Dawn wondered where the instructor was as she smiled slightly at the man, who she assumed was the janitor.

Two of Dawn's second-grade classmates, Carter Barnowl and Scarlett Doveridge, entered the dojo. Ian Parrotti arrived a minute later to round out the new crop of beginners. Each wore a crisp white gi with the fold marks from the packaging still visible.

Sensei returned the broom to the closet and slowly bowed to each new student. Scarlett looked to her mother for guidance, but none was forthcoming.

"Welcome," Sensei said. "Take off your shoes and socks and place them here." He gestured to a shoe rack beside a door leading from the welcome area to the practice floor. "We do not bring dirt from the outside world into our place of learning."

Carter glanced at his father for reassurance as he steadied himself for this new experience.

Sensei stood in the doorframe leading to the dojo and said, "Sometimes the body arrives before the mind. Be here before you pass through this door. Pause momentarily, bring your legs together with your arms at your sides, and bow to the room like this." Sensei bowed a long, slow bow, then stepped onto the dojo floor.

"As you bow, thank the room for allowing you to practice within its walls."

"Thank the room? Why would the room care?" Dawn shrugged.

Sensei walked to the front of the dojo and guided the four students to stand beside each other, separating each by the same amount of space.

"We start each class with a brief meditation. So, Ms. Eagleton, Mr. Barnowl, Ms. Doveridge, and Mr. Parrotti, follow along and do exactly as I do."

With a straight back, Sensei kneeled to one knee, then the other, tucking both legs beneath himself. He rested his hands gently on his thighs, just above the knees, with palms facing down.

The students followed.

"Let your eyes be soft," he continued with a calm authority. "Release the tension in both body and mind. Let the distractions of the outside world fade away and focus on being present here and now."

Each student sat quietly pondering this new experience. Dawn Eagleton was convinced that soon she would beat everyone in the sparring ring. She believed she would quickly progress through the belts and earn her black belt faster than anyone else. It was almost unfair to the rest of the students.

Ian Parrotti's idealism inspired him to think that karate would be easy to learn, and that people would soon sing his praises. He had watched many martial arts movies and, before long, would be punching and kicking like a champ. He was excited for the fun that lay ahead.

Meanwhile, Scarlett Doveridge and Carter Barnowl had concerns. Scarlett was worried that other students were bigger than her and more coordinated. She hoped this wouldn't be too difficult and that this was a place where she could make new friends, though she was concerned that other students wouldn't like her.

Carter considered how much time and hard work it would take to perfect the techniques and pass his first belt test. He compared himself to the other students in the dojo and wondered if he could learn the finer nuances of the techniques. He anticipated the long journey ahead.

"Take one more breath," Sensei instructed. "Open your eyes. Place your left hand gently on the floor before you. Now, your right hand, and bow deeply."

After returning to their seated positions, the students followed Sensei's lead. He placed his left foot in front of him and rose to stand tall with his hands at his side.

White Belt Level 1

As we meet the four students, we glimpse their states of mind. Their wants, fears, past experiences, *and personality* shape their expectations.

Dawn, the Eagle, displayed unfounded confidence. She believes in herself with little evidence to support her assertion. This confidence will serve her well in life, but it may work against her at this moment—her confidence far exceeds her skills.

In karate, this self-deception may cause her to get cocky with opponents far ahead of her ability, and she may attempt things she is not ready to do. Truth be told, if an adult entered my class with, shall I say, an unwavering belief in themselves, my five-foot, one-inch, ninety-pound wife would bring them back to reality after one minute in the sparring ring. There's nothing like someone half your size bringing your ego into balance.

Back to our karate friends. Ian, our resident Parrot, is bursting with optimism. Once again, this will serve him well in life. However, as a martial artist, he may overestimate his abilities and underestimate how much effort is required to learn and refine new techniques. He may need to cultivate a more realistic self-perception and develop greater discipline to avoid distractions.

Scarlett the Dove and Carter the Owl have louder internal critics. Scarlett is concerned about forming genuine relationships. She worries about making new friends and is already questioning if karate is something she can do. The last thing she wants is for others to progress faster than her because it might make her look bad and alienate her from the group. She is also worried that her small size will be a disadvantage no matter how hard she works.

Carter, the Owl, recognizes the complexity of the road ahead and worries that he'll never be able to learn all the intricate techniques. He compares his skill level to Sensei's and wonders if he'll even be able to earn a black belt. How could he ever get that good?

While Dawn and Ian are overly confident, Scarlett and Carter have to build self-esteem. All four students have much to learn.

Level 1 of Personality Intelligence

Individuals at this first stage of Personality Intelligence are like white belts in the martial arts. They are beginning to explore how to use the many aspects of their style.

In this early phase, they likely have poor mechanisms for coping with change or stressful environments. They may deeply internalize their stress or express it wildly. Eagles and Parrots tend to have emotional outbursts, while Doves and Owls have "inbursts," internalizing their stress. Mood swings may be frequent.

People at Level 1 may be highly dependent on others or fundamentally lack trust in those around them and feel they must do everything themselves. They expend a lot of energy grappling with uncomfortable emotions, inner turmoil, and insecurity.

PIQ1 Eagles and Parrots tend to live in the present and neglect the future. This can cause them to act recklessly or selfishly. They either avoid taking responsibility for their actions or blame others for their mistakes.

Conversely, PIQ1 Doves and Owls may regret past actions or worry about the future. They internalize failure and beat themselves up for things they did or feel they should have done. These individuals haven't yet developed confidence, so constructive feedback is difficult to hear and accept. They may react defensively to criticism and be unwilling to acknowledge their areas for improvement.

At this level, individuals are focused on coping rather than thriving, as people aim to relieve stress. Power-driven Eagles prefer to be behind the wheel when others are in the car because not being in control creates tension—driving helps ease that stress. Parrots become uneasy in the presence of negativity, so they instinctively highlight the positive. Doves prioritize stability and will go to great lengths to preserve harmony and maintain the status quo. Owls seek to make the most informed decisions possible, which leads them to gather extensive information before taking action.

With an intense focus on one's needs, individuals at the Unevolved State lack awareness of how their actions affect others. These first-level behaviors won't lead to excellence. At best, people at PIQ1 get by. But remember, this is where everyone begins their journey to becoming their best selves.

Level 1 Fears

Some behaviors stem from our goals and ambitions. At this early stage, however, behaviors often flow from fears and insecurities. The need for stability and the fear of failure or rejection often drive Level 1 actions. These fears can lead people to avoid risks, stay within their comfort zone, and prioritize safety over growth. However, understanding these fears can open the door to self-improvement.

PIQ1 Eagles fear being perceived as soft, weak, or vulnerable. They fear being taken advantage of because they don't like losing. They want to be in charge, as that minimizes the possibility of losing control over situations or outcomes. They might complain about always having to lead school or work projects, but take charge anyway because they believe that is the surest path to success.

Level 1 Parrots fear rejection and not being liked. A lack of social acceptance would devastate a PIQ1 Parrot. Because they don't want to be perceived as dull, uninspiring, or a downer, they try to keep everything positive. FOMO (Fear of Missing Out) is real for Parrots, and I'd bet that a Parrot created the phrase and acronym. In addition, Parrots crave to be seen. If you have a Parrot child, you probably hear them say, "Watch this!" on a regular basis.

Doves fear conflict, dissension, and aggression. The last thing a Dove wants to do is offend someone or hurt their feelings. This causes them to measure their words carefully. Doves also fear sudden change and disruption from the routine. Loss of stability is ungrounding to the Dove. This applies to people, processes, and products. You may find that Doves are so brand loyal that they may use the same product for decades. They may also rotate between several tried-and-true family favorite recipes, eat at the same restaurants, and order the same meals.

PIQ1 Owls fear making mistakes and failing to meet expectations. This causes them to work slowly and carefully to perfect everything they do before declaring it done. Chaos and disorganization are unsettling for an Owl at this level. They crave structure and order, which allows them to achieve their quality standards. The phrase "measure twice and cut once" was surely an Owl invention. Look behind a painting hung by a Parrot. There are probably extra holes from repeated attempts to hammer the right spot. The Owl, meanwhile, used a laser level and a tape measure to nail it on the first attempt.

Too-Much People

Some individuals at Level 1 have amplified their style to such a degree that they are exhausting to be around. Their energy fills the space, leaving no room for anyone else. Simply being in their presence is draining, as one must fight to be heard and seen. These individuals are the Too-Much People.

We've all met a Too-Much Person. Some have an overabundance of one style, while others may display an excess of several. They speak with intensity and deep knowing, causing others to feel that sharing their opinions would be pointless. You might describe them as "a lot" or "extra" or as someone you can only handle in small doses.

These individuals have strong opinions about everything and impose their beliefs on everyone. They often have an overarching view of how things should be, and if you unwittingly disagree with any aspect of their worldview, the battle begins. No topic is too small to debate or correct. They can be obsessive about their interests or beliefs, as if they matter more than anyone else's.

These larger-than-life personalities have limited flexibility and seldom draw from other styles. Consequently, they operate in their style's Red Zone 24/7. On the one hand, this makes it easy to predict how they will react to situations. On the other hand, it takes a lot of energy to avoid sparking these over-the-top reactions.

Too-Much People live at Level 1 of Personality Intelligence, and each style has its own version. The Too-Much Eagle overwhelms others with confidence, while a Too-Much Parrot fills the air with toxic positivity. The Too-Much Dove pulls others into their continuous ebb and flow of emotions, while the Too-Much Owl is the self-imposed enforcer of all rules, stated and unstated.

Sometimes, it is difficult to determine the style of a Too-Much Person, especially when they exhibit a few styles. If they project extreme conviction, you might think they are an Eagle, while their intensity may lead someone else to identify them as a passionate Parrot. Their strong emotions might point to a Dove, but they might, in fact, be a frustrated Eagle. The crushing amount of information they share may suggest they are an Owl, but they might be a Parrot who is trying to persuade you. A Too-Much

Dove or Owl might defend their beliefs aggressively, leading you to assume they are neither of these reserved styles. Figuring out a Too-Much Person's style is tricky, which makes connecting to them challenging.

For a Too-Much person to advance to Level 2, they need to dial back their intensity and bring their behaviors into balance.

How to Deal with People at Level 1

Interacting with individuals in the early stage of their development can often be, as a Parrot might say, "not fun." It takes a nuanced dance of diplomacy to avoid triggering their fears. Just remember, everyone is fighting a battle that you are unaware of. Below are strategies for navigating encounters with people at Level 1.

General Strategies for Encounters with Level 1 People

- *Stay Calm:* Keep your emotions in check. Don't let them provoke an emotional response.
- *Maintain Perspective:* Recognize that their behavior may arise from a longing for validation.
- *Listen Actively:* Validate their feelings and perspectives while gently steering the conversation towards a more balanced exchange.
- *Set Boundaries:* Establish clear boundaries and communicate assertively and respectfully. Let the

individual know when their behavior crosses a line and assert your need for personal space.

- *Avoid Trigger Words:* Use diplomatic language and avoid words that might provoke a negative response, like "No, you're wrong," or "You're being <fill in any negative word>."

- *Don't Take Their Behavior Personally:* Level 1 behaviors reflect the individual's issues and insecurities, not your worth as a person, so, don't allow them to undermine your confidence.

- *Know When to Disengage:* Sometimes, despite our best efforts, individuals at PIQ1 can become overwhelming or draining. It's perfectly acceptable to politely disengage from the conversation or take a step back to recharge.

The following are strategies for interacting with Level 1 people based on their style.

Strategies for Interacting with Level 1 Eagles

- Match their authoritative and bold energy.
- Don't force them into a losing position; make sure they have a choice or an out.
- Accept that they will likely claim victory, even if they lose or are about to lose.
- Don't appear weak or unsure.
- Choose your battles and only fight when it's imperative.

Strategies for Interacting with Level 1 Parrots

- Match their excitement and eager energy.
- Acknowledge the benefit of their hopefulness; then explain how they've missed the mark.
- Avoid pessimistic statements or perspectives.
- Help them shift from generating exciting ideas into action and implementation.
- Be firm that you would like to finish speaking if they cut you off mid-story or mid-sentence.

Strategies for Interacting with Level 1 Doves

- Match their soft and connective energy.
- Don't be overly harsh or blunt.
- Give them time to gather their thoughts.
- Ask them to verbalize their unstated needs, so that they don't assume you understand them.
- Don't mistake their willingness to go along as acceptance of your ideas or decisions.

Strategies for Interacting with Level 1 Owls

- Match their contemplative and reserved energy.
- Back up your opinions with facts and logic.
- Don't invade their personal space.

- Be organized and prepared when presenting ideas or information to them.
- Don't push for an answer too quickly.

Inevitably, you will encounter individuals who are just beginning their Personality Intelligence journey. And yes, many of them are adults! By fostering empathy, setting boundaries, and maintaining perspective, you can navigate these encounters with grace and understanding, fostering meaningful connections while preserving your well-being.

Up Next

In the following chapter, we will see what happens when people progress on the Personality Intelligence journey and reach Level 2.

Chapter 6:
Personality Intelligence Level 2

Discovering the Gifts of Your Style

Six years passed since young Dawn Eagleton, Ian Parrotti, Scarlett Doveridge, and Carter Barnowl bowed into Master Tori's dojo for the first time. After hundreds of classes and tens of thousands of punches and kicks, they had earned their black belts. The next day, the four students tied on their stiff, new belts for the first time. It would take a while to break them in, just as it would take time to adapt to this new rank.

Just before class began, Sensei called the group together. "It is time to cut the cloth," Sensei explained. "Until now, you had to perform each move exactly how I taught it. That was important to help you learn the techniques. But each of you has a different body and a different spirit. As black belts, it is time to honor your individuality. It is time to tailor the cloth to fit you properly. Keep what works and discard the rest. Understood?"

They bellowed a simultaneous "Osu!"—meaning "I understand" and "I will do it."

"Now line up."

Sensei led the class through a brief meditation, warm-up exercises, and a run-through of the basic stances, blocks, and kicks. He then assigned the students to select a kata, or form, and work on it. But before he set them free to work on their katas, he added, "Be the master in you."

In kata training, the students practice various techniques in a choreographed pattern of movements. Katas simulate combat against a series of imaginary opponents.

After a few minutes, Sensei approached Dawn Eagleton. He waited until she finished her kata. Dawn bowed to close the kata and stood at attention, waiting for instructions.

With a firm and directive tone, Sensei began. "Ms. Eagleton, today I share something with you that my instructor shared with me many years ago. My teacher taught me the power of Ikken Hissatsu, or one punch, one victory. Just as the archer requires only one arrow to hit the bullseye, you need only one strike to end the battle. So, make it count."

"Osu!" she replied.

Sensei watched the class for a minute, then approached the next student, Scarlett Doveridge. She always felt a bit self-conscious when Sensei watched her, but that internal voice was getting quieter. Scarlett had selected a different kata from her friend Dawn, and she performed the moves with focused intensity.

After completing the kata, Scarlett came to attention. "Ms. Doveridge," Sensei began with a soft voice. "A river flows smoothly around the rocks. Be like water. Flow like water. Just as water takes the shape of any container it is poured into, remain formless and adapt to your opponent. Be soft and yielding."

Sensei's words, "Be like water," echoed in her mind as if she were giving herself instructions: "Flow like water," she repeated over and over.

Scarlett visualized opponents and pictured herself adapting to their movements. She seamlessly transitioned between techniques as one flowed into the next, moving with grace and fluidity. After a few minutes, Sensei walked by Scarlett and, with the slightest of nods, reassured her that she was doing well. She breathed a sigh of relief as her heart filled with satisfaction.

With Dawn and Scarlett underway, Sensei Tori shifted his attention to Carter Barnowl. Carter was absorbed in his thoughts as he performed the kata. The teacher approached the new black belt student and said, "A samurai's katana sword is sharp and precise as it cuts through the air with its razor-edged blade. When wielding the sword, every movement should be deliberate and accurate. Be sharp like the sword."

Carter replied, "Osu," and endeavored to move with focused intention. He returned to his kata and paid careful attention to each movement, as well as the moves between the moves. After a few minutes, he cut through the distractions, and with clarity of purpose, he focused on his form, timing, and targeting. At one point, he threw a punch and could swear he heard the whoosh of a sword slicing the air.

While all this was happening, Ian Parrotti was busy practicing his favorite kata. It had two jumping moves and a quick spin that he found exciting. When Sensei approached, he couldn't help but smile as he observed pure joy emanating from Ian. Sensei also noticed that Ian was a bit unfocused as he performed the kata.

Sensei waited for him to bow to close the kata. "Mr. Parrotti, you have a vast and unending supply of energy. Just as lightning comes out of nowhere, your attacks can catch your opponent off guard, giving them little time to react. Lightning is fast and explosive. Strikes come without warning and from unexpected directions. Lightning does not hesitate, and neither should you. Strike like lightning."

Ian gave an enthusiastic "Osu" and immediately got to work. "I'm electric," he said, struggling to contain his amusement. He spent the next few minutes trying to be lightning. He moved quickly with sudden movements, changing the speed and angle of his attacks. He was unpredictable. *Ha! Take that*, he thought. *And that. And that. I bet you didn't see that coming!*

After performing the kata, he had a big grin on his face. Then, he laughed out loud when the phrase, "There's no smiling in karate," popped into his head.

Sensei noticed his student's joyful outburst and revealed his delight with the slightest grin. After all, there is no smiling in karate.

Sensei watched his four new black belts working on their respective katas. The katas looked so different and yet so right for each of them. They were cutting the cloth to create the perfect fit. *Today, they are black belts*, thought Sensei Tori.

Developing Your Style

"One size fits all" is a ridiculous claim in almost every aspect of life, from clothing to martial arts techniques to how we treat others. Just picture Simone Biles and Shaquille O'Neal—clearly, one size does *not* fit all. Sensei's advice to "be the master in you" holds the secret to transitioning from Level 1 to Level 2 of Personality Intelligence.

Parents explicitly teach children, "Do what I do." But as we grow, we discover that what works for other individuals does not necessarily work for us. And if we try to emulate someone else, we won't realize our full potential.

Sensei understood that he must teach each student differently. He recognized his role in helping them become the best version of themselves, not the best version of him or someone else. All too often, teachers, parents, coaches, and managers try to turn their charges into themselves.

I remember one day early in my wife's martial arts journey when she was feeling frustrated because she believed she'd never be as powerful as our instructor. His response still sticks with me: "You're right. You will never have my power," he told her. "But with your size and build, one day, you will be so fast I won't be able to touch you." And he was right. She was half his weight and almost a foot shorter, and today, she moves like lightning, and most people can't even get close to her.

Sensei Tori understood that his Eagle student would thrive if she learned to develop power. This nurtured her ability to be decisive and execute under pressure. He taught his Parrot to be fast and unpredictable. This developed his innate ability to think and act quickly and adapt on-the-fly to whatever he might encounter.

As for the Dove, Sensei guided her to flow, which supported her soft and yielding style. Meanwhile, Sensei taught his Owl student to be accurate and move with intention. He reinforced his ability to meticulously pay attention to every detail.

Sensei didn't try to make his students conform to a standard image of excellence. He honored each of their true natures and helped develop their natural gifts. As you develop your Personality Intelligence, remember the lesson that Sensei taught his students: Be the master in you, not the master in someone else.

Level 2 of Personality Intelligence

Over time, most individuals shift from the Unevolved State to the Typical State. This developmental process can be born of intentional behavioral change or through maturity as we age. Some learn quickly, and others learn slowly.

Of course, some remain stuck in Level 1 throughout their lives. But if you think it's stressful to interact with these folks, imagine the battle waging within them! While some struggles are visible, others remain hidden beneath the surface, masked by smiles or blank expressions. These individuals may have experienced trauma or may lack accountability by blaming others or circumstances for their lot in life.

Those who remain at Level 1 can frustrate those who have advanced to Level 2, as they remind them of an earlier version of themselves they are working to leave behind. *I've learned not to behave like that—why haven't they?*

This is why a parent with a child of the same style, such as an Eagle parent with an Eagle child, can quickly become annoyed. The parent may have learned that honesty does not require sharing every thought, such as a dislike for a spouse's outfit. So, when the child mirrors traits that the parent doesn't feel particularly proud of, feelings of shame arise. The parent unrealistically wants their child to advance to Level 2 without experiencing the lessons that everyone must first learn in Level 1.

In Level 1, people regularly overuse their strengths, and their style works against them. The traits that could have been their greatest asset are their greatest liability. In Level 2, Red Zone behaviors are exhibited under stress or when triggered by earlier trauma. Old hardwiring never goes away. We just overlay new hardwiring over the old, and when we are stressed, old patterns kick in.

When this happens, the person at Level 2 may regret their behaviors or feel frustrated that they reverted to old patterns. But this is how learning occurs: two steps forward, one step back. The key is to keep moving forward.

When someone reaches Level 2 of Personality Intelligence, they are a beginner all over again, like the black belt. They have developed a new set of automatic reactions that serve them better than at Level 1. And now, they must relearn how to exist in the world with these new responses.

At this stage, the inner critic gets quieter, self-deception yields to a more realistic view of oneself, and self-esteem grows stronger. Ineffective reactions give way to more thoughtful responses. Daily stress is lower, and individuals engage in far less conflict. Relationships become healthier, and the individuals become more productive.

Those who operate in the Typical State engage in positive social interactions. They typically understand and conform to societal norms and communicate well enough to get by. They generally work effectively with others and display a reasonable degree of professionalism. They are proficient enough to systematically work on tasks, meet goals, and create satisfying careers.

Use Your Strengths, But Don't Overuse Them

At a healthy level, our style allows us to cultivate strong relationships and build successful careers, but when we push our style into the Red Zone, our strengths become our weaknesses. To use an accounting analogy, our greatest assets become our greatest liabilities.

We are the worst version of ourselves in the Red Zone. At PIQ2, this typically occurs when we are under stress or out of balance. At work, long hours or times of change can elicit this response. At home, financial or relationship issues can bring out Red Zone behaviors. Even positive changes such as getting married, having a child, or moving to a new home can cause our style to kick into overdrive.

When this happens, Eagles become aggressive, stubborn, and demanding. They may overstep boundaries and steamroll others. Their communication devolves into abrupt and abrasive interactions that can be offensive. Their take-charge leadership skills become

domineering as their drive to do things immediately leads to reckless behaviors and bad decisions. They can regain balance by slowing down and regrounding themselves.

When Parrots enter the Red Zone, feathers fly! They become unrealistic, manipulative, excitable, scattered, overly self-promoting, and possibly even delusional. Their stories can become grandiose and over-exaggerated. They may underestimate their available time, miss deadlines, and disregard facts by overly relying on their gut. Parrots who push their style to the extreme must take a step back and look at themselves and their challenges objectively. This will enable them to speak and act with thought instead of impulse.

As for the Dove, is there no greater call than for more love in this world? Sure, but even compassion pushed too far can become smothering. While Eagles become aggressive and arrogant, Doves become passive and insecure. Doves in the Red Zone consistently place the needs of others before their own. They become dependent, permissive, fearful, and overly accommodating. Doves in overuse mode may struggle to maintain the status quo, rather than be open to the possibilities of what could be. They need to reestablish boundaries and remember to address their own needs before attempting to accommodate everyone else.

For Owls, the quest for quality and accuracy turns into perfectionism. They become pessimistic, indecisive, and rigid—overly critical of themselves and those around them. Their rigorous information requirements can create analysis paralysis as they fail to make decisions or act. Owls in the Red Zone need to ease up on their pursuit of perfection, work within existing time constraints, and do their best with available resources.

At a healthy level, our strengths drive our success. But if you want to get to Level 3, don't overuse them.

Don't Try to Change Other People

Advancing through Level 2 requires a high degree of acceptance, not just for ourselves but for everyone we meet. We must acknowledge that each person is on their own journey and respect their path.

There's an expression often attributed to Mark Twain: "Don't try to teach a pig to sing. It will frustrate you and annoy the pig." When we try to change those closest to us, we imply that they should *be* someone different because we do not value or respect who they are today. And it degenerates from there.

If you're a parent, and you constantly try to correct and change your child's style of behavior, your child may think that they aren't good enough—that you don't love them for who they are. If you are a manager, your direct report may feel like they need to act like someone else to keep their job. That's exhausting—not to mention distracting from their work goals.

You can't custom design someone else's style. Whether that person is a child or a spouse or a team member at work, you can't force them to be who they are not. When you do that, you can negatively affect their self-esteem, generate anxiety, and create an identity crisis. Instead, help people be the best version of themselves, not the best version of you.

How to Interact More Effectively with People at Level 2

Individuals with Personality Intelligence know how to interact with people of other styles. The following are tips for interacting with people of each style as they evolve.

Strategies for Interacting with Level 2 Eagles

- Be no-nonsense, concise, and get to the point quickly.
- Display confidence in your opinions and decisions.
- Focus on results, tangible outcomes, and benefits.
- Don't take bluntness personally, as it isn't intended to offend but to be efficient.
- Recognize their successes and achievements.

Strategies for Interacting with Level 2 Parrots

- Match their energy by being engaging, upbeat, and energetic.
- Encourage creativity by allowing them to think outside the box and express their ideas.
- Allow time for connecting through storytelling.
- Give praise and recognition to celebrate their successes.
- Be flexible and spontaneous, as Parrots do not like to follow strict plans or routines.

Strategies for Interacting with Level 2 Doves

- Be gentle and patient and avoid rushing or pressuring them.
- Listen actively, as Doves value being heard and understood.
- Create a calm, peaceful, and stable environment with minimal conflict.
- Provide clear guidance and expectations to help them feel secure in their role or tasks.
- Avoid aggressive behavior, as Doves shy away from confrontation.

Strategies for Interacting with Level 2 Owls

- Be prepared with all relevant facts, plans, timelines, and expectations, as they may ask in-depth questions.
- Be patient with decision-making, as Owls tend to be cautious and deliberate.
- Avoid emotional appeals by prioritizing facts over emotions.
- Respect their independence, as Owls often prefer working alone to ensure accuracy.
- Appreciate their thoroughness by showing appreciation for their detailed efforts

Up Next

While most people remain at Level 2 and only have glimpses of Level 3, anyone has the potential to master their style. Let's return to the dojo to see how this transformation takes shape.

Chapter 7:
Personality Intelligence Level 3

Master Your Style

Ten years passed since Dawn, Ian, Scarlett, and Carter first entered the dojo. They would soon be heading off to college, and tonight was one of their last remaining classes together.

Sensei Tori stood in front of the room to call the class together. Today, they would focus on sparring.

Following the opening meditation and a series of warm-up exercises, Sensei took the four black belts to the front of the room while one of the brown belts worked with the remaining students in the back. Sensei stood tall and said, "As black belts, you have been shaping your techniques, cutting through the fabric of tradition to make them your own. Mastery isn't just about skill—it's about cultivating balance. That is the true path."

Sensei gestured for Scarlett to join him. The old master assumed a fighting stance and guided his student to do the same.

Sensei looked into Scarlett's eyes and simply said, "Soft," indicating they should move gently. This created a common ground for both partners to move with the same intensity.

"Do not acknowledge points," instructed Sensei. "Move as if we are one."

Curiously, before they began, Sensei turned to Dawn and firmly said, "Watch."

The pair bowed to each other, and Sensei said, "Hajime," signaling for the exercise to begin.

Scarlett followed Sensei's lead and moved like water. Like a flock of starlings flying in a synchronized rhythm, they moved as one. As Sensei shifted his weight forward, Scarlett shifted her weight backward. It was a breathtaking display—an elegant, slow-motion dance.

After about two minutes, Sensei quietly said, "Yame," signaling to stop.

They bowed to each other, and Scarlett lined up with her fellow students. Sensei returned his gaze to Dawn and asked, "Did you see how we moved? Remember."

He let his words hang in the air before calling Dawn to join him. With a strong voice, he instructed, "For a moment, put aside what you just saw and show me what you have."

This time, before they began, Sensei looked at Scarlett and without a word, conveyed that she should pay careful attention.

Even before they began, Dawn radiated intensity and the conviction to win. She immediately threw an explosive punch at Sensei's head, which he easily blocked with firm force. In response,

Sensei delivered a front kick, piercing her defense, stopping just an eighth of an inch from her abdomen. Undeterred, the student ramped up her intensity, launching several aggressive attacks. Sensei met her intensity with equal force.

After going back and forth, Sensei called the match to an end. They bowed, and Dawn lined back up with her peers.

Sensei immediately turned to Scarlett and asked, "Did you see what we did?"

She replied with a booming, "Osu!"

Sensei then turned to Dawn and Scarlett and told them he wanted them to spar each other. He then guided Scarlett to spar with power and force and Dawn to flow smoothly and gently.

Dawn started to raise her hand as if she were about to ask a question to which Sensei immediately responded, "No questions. You know what to do."

The two students moved to the side of the dojo and tried to embody the energy of the other. It was challenging at first, but soon, Dawn began to gently guide Scarlett's powerful punches and kicks aside, as Scarlett showed fierce intensity.

Across the room, Sensei Tori turned to Carter and signaled for him to come forward. Carter promptly approached and stood at attention.

Sensei looked him in the eyes and said, "Medium," indicating they should move at half-power. Carter assumed his best front stance and placed his arms in the ready position. This time, before he began, Sensei glanced at Ian. He knew that he was just told to watch carefully.

The match began and both martial artists moved with precision. Every movement was a calculated blend of strategy and skill. Their accurate strikes were grounded by intricate footwork. They precisely delivered punches and kicks, targeting vulnerable points with minimal wasted motion. Their stance was stable and balanced, allowing them to move smoothly in and out of range. Each technique was so perfectly executed that it seemed almost choreographed.

After the match ended, Sensei caught Ian's eye, and a smile lit up his face. With a nod, he called him to the front of them.

Ian was thoroughly delighted. Even before they began, the air was electric. Sensei looked at Carter, though he was already focused intently on what was happening. The match started with an energetic flurry of attacks from both of them. Their movements were dramatic, quick, and unpredictable and their kicks almost theatrical. They sparred as if they were dancing on hot coals and both seemed to thoroughly enjoy the interaction. It was fun to watch.

With Scarlett and Dawn paired off in one corner, Sensei instructed Carter and Ian to partner together and practice what they just witnessed. But to their surprise, Sensei told Carter to spar with speed and spontaneity and Ian to move with careful precision.

It took a few minutes for them to get in their partner's rhythm, but before long, they were doing it. Carter moved quickly and even added some playful taunts. Ian was patient and only attacked when the perfect target was available.

After about fifteen minutes, Sensei gathered the four students together and said, "You have each cut your own cloth to make the martial arts fit your body, mind, and spirit. But to truly master the techniques, you must bring what you have learned into balance. To know hard, you must also know soft. To know speed, you must also understand power. There is much you can learn from each other. You are not just learning a different way to fight. You are learning a different way to live."

Sensei bowed to the students who understood that the martial arts are not just about physical mastery but also about embracing their journey and forging their unique path.

After the class concluded, the four friends weren't ready to part, so Ian proposed they grab some ice cream, and everyone agreed. They had much to discuss.

What Happened in the Dojo?

We just observed Level 3 of Personality Intelligence in action. Did you notice how each student displayed their personality in their sparring match with Sensei? Scarlett effortlessly employed her Dove strengths as she flowed softly and fluidly. Dawn, the Eagle, was naturally assertive, competitive, and intense. Carter's Owl abilities allowed him to be accurate and calculated, while Ian brought excitement and flair to the match.

At first, Sensei let their natural strengths come through, knowing that true effectiveness arises when individuals operate from their inherent style. That's where authentic power lives. As they sparred with their instructor, we saw each student at their best—fully embracing their unique abilities and beginning to unlock their true potential.

However, Sensei Tori also challenged his students to step beyond their comfort zones by embracing the gifts of the opposite style. He understood that true growth doesn't come from staying rooted solely in one's natural tendencies but from learning to adapt and evolve. Doves can gain confidence and assertiveness from Eagles, just as Eagles can benefit from the patience and empathy of Doves. Likewise, Owls can be inspired by the creativity and spontaneity of Parrots, while Parrots can learn focus and precision from Owls.

Sensei Tori recognized that real mastery requires balance—the ability to draw from both sides of the spectrum. By encouraging his students to explore these contrasting energies, he helped them temper their dominant traits and become more well-rounded, resilient individuals. It was not about changing who they were but about expanding who they could become.

In doing so, Sensei Tori wasn't just teaching them how to spar. He was guiding them toward a deeper understanding of themselves. Through balance, they could access a fuller expression of their power and move through the world with greater wisdom and grace.

Level 3 of Personality Intelligence

At PIQ3, individuals have learned to balance the opposites of their style. Consider Old Faithful in Yellowstone National Park.

Its stillness before an eruption makes the spectacle even more thrilling. If it were a constant stream of water shooting into the air, people might watch for a moment and lose interest. The anticipation, the contrast between quiet and explosion, is what creates excitement.

Similarly, mastering one's personality lies in knowing when to utilize one's gifts and when to employ their complement. Just as a bright light seems brighter in darkness, exhibiting a strength's opposite allows it to shine brighter.

Eagles and Doves are opposites, while Parrots and Owls are opposites. Consider the diagram below: the horizontal axis ranges from task-oriented to people-oriented. The vertical axis stretches from fast-paced and verbal at the top to even-paced and reserved at the bottom. You may have noticed that I renamed William Marston's original axis labels here to make them intuitive and practical.

Antagonistic and Favorable are now Task and People. Active and Passive are Fast-paced, Verbal and Even-Paced, Reserved.

The Eagle is in the top left, the Parrot in the top right, the Dove in the bottom right, and the Owl in the bottom left. Notice that the diagonal styles have completely different axis labels. This is why they are opposites.

If you've read my book *The Chameleon*, you may recall that I prefer the word *complement* to *opposite*. The idea of opposites suggests a conflict or a contradiction, whereas a complement emphasizes how the qualities of one style fill in the gaps of or add value to the other. *Complement* highlights the idea of mutual

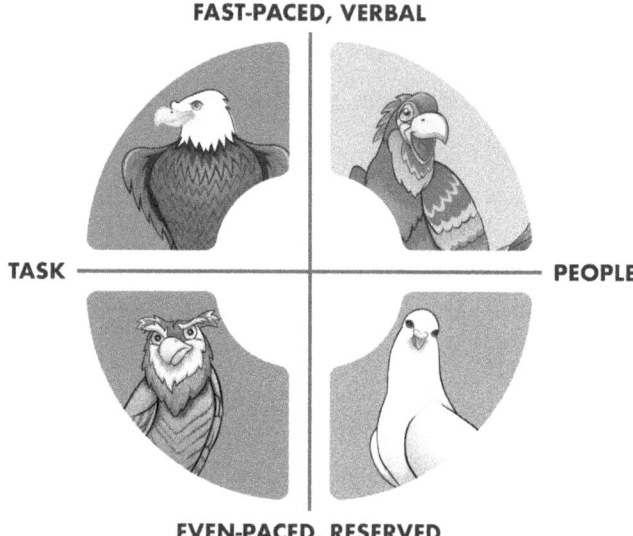

enhancement, where both styles work together to create a stronger, more balanced individual.

Master Eagles radiate confidence, but they temper it with humility, avoiding arrogance. They know when to lead decisively and when to step back, trusting others to take the reins.

Parrots at this level captivate others with storytelling, yet they balance talking with listening, ensuring others feel heard. They flourish when juggling multiple priorities and can also zero in on what matters most to drive meaningful results.

PIQ3 Doves are generous and nurturing, but they have learned to care for themselves, understanding that self-care is not selfish. They willingly help others avoid painful situations but also allow people to learn hard lessons that will benefit them later in life.

Level 3 Owls are skilled at digging into the details but can also see the big-picture vision. They excel in planning, but they recognize that action must follow thought, knowing when to strategize and when to execute.

People in the Master State possess a profound understanding of their innate gifts and have honed the ability to leverage them effectively. As we just witnessed in the dojo, they also bring their gifts into balance with their opposite traits. This provides a remarkable level of self-regulation. Eagles who can be quick to anger, stay calm and centered like a Dove in stressful times. Parrots who can become scattered when things go awry, maintain focus like an Owl. Doves who can get lost in emotions and lose sight of the goal can target the key actions that will ultimately achieve success and alleviate the stressor. And Owls who can get lost in planning can make quick decisions like a Parrot.

This empowers individuals at this level to perform at their best, even in the face of adversity. The very situations that once triggered unproductive behaviors in their Unevolved State now serve as catalysts for growth and excellence.

Witnessing a Level 3 person in action is like watching a master craftsman carve a breathtaking sculpture. A beginner may use the same tools and techniques, but the outcome will never be the same. At Level 3, individuals bring their strengths into harmony with their opposites, elevating their natural gifts to the highest level of Personality Intelligence.

Let Go of False Beliefs

People at Level 1, and to a lesser degree, those at Level 2, hold inaccurate perceptions of themselves and others. Their false beliefs limit their growth; however, those who have mastered their style transcend these misconceptions. They tell stories about themselves that are grounded in truth and reality.

PIQ3 Eagles express humility and transcend the notion that their priorities are more important than those of everyone else. They think win-win instead of win-lose and find ways to make everyone successful and happy. Healthy rivalry inspires third-level Eagles to strive for their best, and they believe that even in defeat, they will be respected. Their self-esteem is no longer based on outside achievement, as they are secure within themselves and humble about their success.

Parrots accept that they don't always have to be seen in a positive light. There's a quote commonly attributed to Winston Churchill, "When you're 20, you care what everyone thinks. When you're 40, you stop caring what everyone thinks. When you're 60, you realize no one was ever thinking about you in the first place." PIQ3 Parrots carry this spirit and live independently of the opinions of others. They have a sense of realism and are not put off by pessimism or negativity. They do not carry the burden of finding the bright side of everything.

Doves at Level 3 no longer base their self-worth on how much they do for those in their life. They let go of the thought that they will be judged as selfish if they place their needs above others. They feel whole and worthy of being loved because of who they are, not what they do for others. Doves at Level 3 are comfortable in the spotlight and willing to advocate for what they want. They let go of the false belief that they will be disliked and perceived as disruptive if they engage in conflict.

Level 3 Owls accept their flaws and overcome the notion that it's unacceptable to make mistakes. They understand that they don't have to be perfect, and they won't be judged solely on something that is not their best work. Master-level Owls release the idea that they will not be valued if they are not perfect, and they stop measuring themselves by their flaws. They see themselves as whole people and accept the good and the bad. Overall, they no longer conflate what they do with who they are.

Advancing Through the Levels

Now that you know the three levels, let's see a real-life example of progression from Level 1 to Level 2 to Level 3.

When Richard Branson dropped out of high school in the 1960s, the headmaster of his UK boarding school's parting words for the fifteen-year-old were, "Congratulations, Branson. I predict that you will either go to prison or become a millionaire." He was right on both counts. It was a prediction befitting a Level 1 Parrot with enormous potential, both constructive and destructive.

Branson wasn't cut out for British boarding school life. Bored with the classroom experience and struggling with undiagnosed dyslexia, Branson was underestimated by his peers. "I was seen as the dumbest person in school," he remembered. He hated how the school micromanaged his life, with mandatory church attendance, faux military marches with rifles, and a tradition where younger students played servant to upperclassmen. He dropped out to start *Student* magazine. The publication operated in a friend's basement, fueled by drugs, sex, and partying.

In 1970, he founded Virgin as a mail-order record business, opening his first retail shop in 1971. His Parrot knack for curating an experience and community turned it into a popular hangout for music customers. However, as Level 1 Parrots are prone to do, Branson started to take massive financial risks, even though *Student* was unprofitable and Virgin barely supported Branson and his business partner. As an influential Parrot, he somehow convinced a bank to lend him tens of thousands of pounds to open a recording studio, in an old mansion that hosted raucous parties.

Plagued by mounting debt, Branson came up with a profitable but illegal scheme to avoid paying import tariffs on foreign records; he was caught by UK authorities. Said Branson, "I had always got away with breaking rules before. In those days I felt that I could do no wrong and that, even if I did, I wouldn't get caught." For a Level 1 Parrot who views laws as suggested guidelines, his plan attempted to correct for the consequences of too much fun and risk, and it went horribly wrong.

The fallout and a night in jail marked a turning point; Branson became serious about building a real business, still with Parrot flair and pizazz. He vowed to never again do anything that would embarrass the business, and he brought on his cousin, Simon Draper, to professionalize Virgin and help operate it soundly. Often, people need a major setback, failure, or disappointment to ignite that shift and this was the beginning of his transition from Level 1 to Level 2.

That maturation paid off. Virgin got back into the record business, created their own label, and went on to launch innovative and overlooked artists including Mike Oldfield, the Sex Pistols, and Boy George. By the end of the 1970s, Virgin was a formidable record label, and Branson owned Necker Island in the Caribbean. It wasn't the soundest financial decision at the time, but it all ended up okay.

Firmly a Level 2 Parrot in the 1980s, Branson expanded Virgin into a global business empire, seemingly able to create a business in any industry. His decision to launch Virgin Atlantic airline in 1984 seemed like lunacy to many, but Branson specifically wanted to be in industries where customers were disgruntled. He knew he could make the experience marvelously fun, human, and memorable. That's a Parrot business in action.

But remember, at Level 2, an individual's style can occasionally get them in trouble and an unchecked Parrot with a growing fortune is a recipe for danger. In the '80s, Branson embarked on a series of ballooning adventures that involved crossing oceans and, eventually, circumnavigating the world. Ultimately, he had to be rescued by helicopter four separate times and almost got himself and his teammates killed. And while he'd tell himself in the moment to never do anything like it again if he survived, he didn't keep those promises until the 2000s.

By 1984, Virgin had over $200 million in revenues, and by 1986, some $500 million in debt. A Level 2 Parrot at this point, Branson finally hired a professional finance staff, who were stunned that he'd managed to run the company with such a haphazardly constructed financial infrastructure. They guided Branson towards incorporating some Owl detail, process, and discipline.

To be clear, Branson continued to have loads of fun. For the launch of the ill-fated Virgin Brides stores in 1996, Branson appeared in a bridal gown for the press and cameras. Several publicity stunts for Virgin Mobile involved Branson and Co. in their birthday suits. Other stunts involved Branson driving a tank through New York and flashing the press with underpants that read "stiff competition."

It can be difficult to pinpoint exactly when a person begins the transition from Level 2 to 3. For Branson, it likely began in 1990, after Saddam Hussein's Iraq invaded Kuwait. Tens of thousands of refugees fled to Jordan, and Branson, disturbed by the violence and injustice, contacted Queen Rania of Jordan to see how he could help. Two days later, a Virgin 747 loaded with blankets, food, and medical supplies landed in Jordan.

Branson later orchestrated a deal with Hussein to trade medical supplies for four hundred hostages held by the Iraqi dictator. At Hussein's request, Branson flew to Iraq personally, at a massive risk to himself and Virgin Atlantic, which couldn't get the flight insured, and returned with the four hundred hostages.

Around this time, we begin to see more Level 3 Parrot in his business decisions. When an opportunity arose to sell Virgin Music, Branson felt reluctant to let go of his original passion project. "Decided to go for the conservative route for the first time in my life," he wrote in his diary. Branson had channeled enough Owl to make what, in retrospect, was a sound decision. And his spirits soon recovered: "For the first time in my life," he said, "I had enough money to fulfill my wildest dreams."

Today, Branson is worth over $2.6 billion, and 45 companies operate under the Virgin Group brand. They range from airlines, hotels, and betting to telecom, finance, and space travel. His current business philosophy shows a Parrot appetite for exploration with an Owl's knack for controlled experimentation: "I'm a great believer in just trying things in a small way, putting a toe in the water...we'll try things, and then if it looks like we've misjudged, we'll quietly move on to something different," Branson told *Entrepreneur*. "But if it looks like it's worth putting more fuel on the target, we'll keep it going."

The title of his 2006 book, *Screw It, Let's Do It,* is not just an embodiment of his style, it might be the most Parrot book title of all time!

Four Steps to Mastering Level 3

Understanding your personality is only the beginning. Real transformation comes from intentional action. If you're looking to evolve your personality, take time to reflect and put the following steps into action.

1. Recognize Your Default Patterns

    Each of us has natural tendencies that shape how we think, communicate, and behave. Take stock of your signature strengths. The more you understand your innate gifts, the more effectively you will be able to capitalize on them. By identifying your behavioral patterns, you gain the power to shift from autopilot to purposeful action.

Start by asking yourself:

- When am I at my best?
- What behaviors energize and deplete me?
- What tasks allow my strengths to shine?
- How do I typically respond under pressure?
- What five adjectives would others use to describe me?

2. Lean Into Your Strengths, But Don't Overuse Them

As Carl Jung said, "The brighter the light, the darker the shadow." Your strengths allow you to shine, but they inhibit success when overused. Examine each of your strengths and identify what they would look like in the Red Zone—the point where your greatest assets work against you.

Notice how confidence can turn into arrogance, enthusiasm into recklessness, kindness into self-sacrifice, and precision into paralysis. Recognizing these tipping points will allow you to be at your best, where your strengths remain assets rather than liabilities. Mastery comes from using your natural gifts at the highest level.

3. Embrace the Opposite of Your Signature Strengths

True mastery of personality comes not just from leveraging your strengths but from embracing their opposites. If you're naturally bold and decisive, there's power in practicing patience and collaboration. If you're highly social and expressive, moments of quiet reflection can bring clarity. If you're nurturing and peace-seeking, stepping into assertiveness can strengthen your influence. And if you're analytical and detail-oriented, learning to trust intuition can unlock new possibilities.

By incorporating qualities that complement your strengths, you become more grounded, adaptable, and effective. This not only enhances your natural abilities but also empowers you to connect and thrive beyond your default style.

4. Turn Awareness Into Action

To truly master your personality, you must apply the insights from Steps 1, 2, and 3 in real-world applications. During stressful moments, pause and choose your response rather than reacting on impulse. During conflicts, be mindful of when your style may be at odds with someone else's and adjust to create better alignment. Seek out people and tasks that allow your personality to shine.

The more you practice and apply the skills of Personality Intelligence, the more natural and effortless it becomes.

How to Deal with People at Level 3:

To be clear, we don't have to figure out how to deal with people who have mastered their style; they have to figure out how to deal with us.

Most of us would do anything to spend more time with someone at Level 3. If they are a parent or sibling, you likely feel blessed to have them in your life. If this person is your boss, you are probably very loyal to them, as you believe they have helped you in immeasurable ways.

You don't deal with them. You learn from them. So, be open. Watch how they display their style authentically. Notice how they engage in meaningful conversations and are present to those around them.

If you are lucky enough to know someone who has reached the third level of Personality Intelligence, spend as much time with them as you can and appreciate your good fortune!

Up Next

There is one more level to go. Let's move forward and see what happens when someone has mastered all the styles.

Chapter 8:
Personality Intelligence Level 4

The Grandmaster

Dawn, Ian, Scarlett, and Carter returned to their hometown after college and continued training with Sensei Tori. Almost a decade had passed since graduation, and each focused on building their careers, putting in long hours and working hard to impress their employers.

Sensei Tori had been unwell for several months, so the four friends alternated leading karate classes in his absence. One day, as they bowed into the dojo, they found him sweeping the floor, just as he had on the first day they met him and before every class since. Despite his frailty, he still projected an unwavering presence.

The four friends donned their gis and tied their fraying black belts.

The old master began, "I asked you to join me here today as I do not know how much time I have left, and there is one final lesson I wish to impart before I am called home."

The students felt thankful to be with their teacher and sorrowful that their time with him would soon come to an end.

Sensei continued, "I humbly ask for one more chance to be your teacher. And don't go easy on me. I've forgotten more than you know," he said with a playful grin.

He gestured for his students to surround him at the four cardinal points of a compass. Sensei spoke calmly, "Attack with everything you have, but do not signal when a point is scored. If you feel that an attack would have taken out your arm and it can no longer be used, do not use it. Step out of the ring if you believe you've been struck with a finishing blow. I will do the same. No contact. One inch from the target counts as a hit. A little less for me," he said with a wink.

They bowed, and just before Sensei called out "Hajime!" to start the battle, he paused and said with a knowing tone, "There are times when you must meet fire with fire."

Ian struck first, second, and third. Loud shouts accompanied each flurry of punches and kicks. He tried to distract his teacher with a sneaky blow, but Sensei was too fast. Before Ian knew it, he was hit with two punches, one of which was a finishing blow. He left the ring.

Dawn was next. She was searching for an opening to end this on her terms. *There!* she thought. Sensei had left the side of his body near his floating rib open. A single sidekick was all she needed. If it met its target, that would do it.

Sensei sidestepped her aggressive strike and delivered one punch to her temple. Dawn bowed to her Sensei in defeat.

The old master turned to Carter, who had been biding his time, waiting for the perfect opening. He waited patiently to find a weakness but could not find one. Slowly and methodically, he watched as Sensei shifted his body. That's when Carter saw it. Sensei lowered his hands, leaving his chin vulnerable. Carter threw a backfist to the point of Sensei's chin, but before he knew what was happening, he felt the slight tap of Sensei's knuckles on his stomach. Carter bowed out of the ring, wondering how Sensei did that.

Only Scarlett remained. Rather than rush to attack, she held her ground and remained in a defensive posture. Sensei did the same. She waited for the master to strike, but he did not. For what seemed like an eternity, they stood there, neither of them moving. He soon approached with grace and subtlety, testing her defenses until she had no choice but to engage. When she did, the master's movements were soft and flowing until she felt a light tap on her back, signaling her defeat. How he got there, she had no idea.

Sensei stood alone in the center of the ring and called his students to stand before him. "What just happened?" he asked.

"You kicked our butts," Ian joked.

Everyone laughed. Even Sensei hinted at a smile. They gathered their composure and Scarlett said, "You sparred each of us differently. You were soft and fluid with me, precise and sharp with Carter, fast and energetic with Ian, and powerful with Dawn. I can't help but notice that you reflected our own sparring styles back to us."

Sensei grinned.

"To add to that," Carter noted, "you matched our personalities."

"Yes!" Sensei exclaimed. "I merged my spirit with yours and became a mirror reflecting your true essence."

Everyone nodded in understanding.

"How did it feel to spar me?" Sensei asked.

"Despite the outcome, I thought it was fun," said Ian.

"Connecting," answered Scarlett. "I felt a bond with you as we flowed together."

"Really?" Dawn asked, laughing. "Sensei could have killed me with his power, and you thought it was nice!"

Carter added, "I liked the sharpness of Sensei's techniques. It was a clean sparring match where form mattered."

"My work is nearly through. But before we go, we have one more battle to fight. Sometimes, you must fight fire with water."

They all gave a universal look of confusion, but there was no time to think. They bowed and the match commenced. Sensei lunged fast at Carter, landing two front kicks to his torso and a roundhouse to his head, followed with a punch to the nose. Carter knew he was done.

Sensei then turned to Scarlett. She began to circle him like water flowing around a rock, but his intensity was overwhelming. Before she knew what was happening, he lunged towards her, reaching his left palm behind her head and pulling it into his right forearm. The sleeve of his gi barely skimmed her nose. Two down.

Dawn aggressively advanced on her teacher, but Sensei responded with grace and flowed around the attacks. Dawn tried to make each technique the deciding blow, but Sensei remained calm. Instead of striking, the teacher focused on defense, keeping his stance grounded and his energy soft. Each time Dawn launched a punch or kick, Sensei would step aside, deflecting the force with minimal effort.

Sensei's approach gradually wore down his opponent. Finally, when Dawn was losing steam, he sidestepped her charging attack and punched her in the temple as she passed by. She bowed out of the ring.

Ian was overflowing with anticipation. He knew this was his last chance to defeat his teacher and would savor every moment. Sensei stood calm and observant while Ian released a barrage of flashy strikes and spinning kicks, trying to overwhelm him with speed and unpredictability.

Sensei didn't counter every attack—instead, he observed, calculating the right opportunity to counter. When Ian threw a punch to Sensei's face, the teacher struck a pressure point on Ian's arm, making it go numb. Then, when he threw a front kick to his teacher's stomach, his teacher found the exact point on his shin that made his leg tingle and buckle beneath his weight. After Sensei took out Ian's other arm, Sensei threw a punch to the point of Ian's chin, ending the fight. The four students were defeated again.

The group licked their wounds and stood before their teacher, who began, "At times, you must adapt to your opponent's style, moving in harmony with who they are and what they do. As you become one with them, you synchronize your movements with them. Other times, you must embrace the opposite, using contrast to your advantage."

The students nodded.

"How did this round feel?" asked Sensei.

"I think I liked your softer side," Scarlett said.

"That was much more difficult," Carter acknowledged.

"I agree," Dawn replied.

"Me too," Ian added.

Sensei continued. "Meeting people where they are creates unity. But it's not always what is called for. Just as yin and yang are entwined in an eternal dance, fire sometimes needs water to temper its power, and water needs the sun's heat to return to the sky so it can fall upon the Earth and nourish the crops. Balance is nature's way. You must learn to adapt to anyone or anything you encounter. Understand?"

"Osu!" the group enthusiastically replied in unison.

Sensei drew a long, slow breath. "It has been my honor to be your teacher. I will live on through each of you."

The class ended with an extended meditation, and the students quietly reflected, grateful to be in the presence of this teacher who had profoundly shaped their lives. They knew they would miss him deeply.

What Happened in the Dojo?

We just witnessed the highest level of Personality Intelligence in action. If someone at Level 3 is a master of Personality Intelligence, someone at Level 4 is a grandmaster. Sensei Tori was a Chameleon, changing his style depending on the situation. In the first round,

Sensei matched the style of each opponent. He fought Dawn as an Eagle, Ian as a Parrot, Scarlett as a Dove, and Carter as an Owl.

Sometimes, aligning with an opponent's style is essential. This may involve adopting their techniques, rhythm, and mindset. Doing so fosters understanding and cooperation, allowing for smoother interactions and a greater sense of awareness. This is especially true with partners in the sparring ring.

In the second round, however, Sensei responded to his students by using the opposite of their fighting styles. He sparred Dawn, the Eagle, as a Dove. Conversely, he sparred Scarlett, the Dove, as an Eagle. He fought Carter, the Owl, as a Parrot, and Ian, the Parrot, as an Owl.

If someone is fast, you slow down. If they are patient, you attack quickly. This can work in the sparring ring and in life.

At Level 4 Personality Intelligence, Sensei Tori embodied all four styles. He understood that being skilled in one approach is not enough. True mastery lies in the ability to adapt fluidly to the situation. This principle of alignment and opposition extends far beyond the dojo. In all our interactions, whether personal or professional, command of all four styles can bring success and fulfillment beyond our wildest dreams.

Level 4 of Personality Intelligence

With the full range of behaviors in their arsenal, Chameleons are versatile in their personal and professional interactions. They know when to match someone's style and when to pour water on a burning fire. They can solve problems and lead with the varied perspectives of the four styles. Ultimately, the Chameleon's ability to adapt and make others feel understood sets them apart.

Chameleons are like the utility players on a baseball team. They can play multiple positions rather than one specific role. Utility players are valuable because they add depth to the roster, allowing managers to rest regular starters or fill in for injured players without significantly weakening the team's overall performance.

Anyone can display any behavior, but Chameleons do so effortlessly. For most people, working out of their style is draining and stressful. Not so for Chameleons. They are not locked into the automatic responses of their natural style; adaptability *is* their natural state.

Chameleons possess a healthy foundation of self-awareness and self-acceptance, as they understand their natural tendencies and areas for growth. They also have a healthy level of self-esteem, yet they are humble. They are secure in displaying any style without losing their sense of self. They feel secure in who they are, so when they adapt to what is needed, it comes from a genuine desire to enhance relationships rather than from insecurity or people-pleasing. Strong self-esteem empowers them to move fluidly between styles while maintaining authenticity and integrity.

Since Chameleons can embody any style with the right intensity, they can create balance in any situation. PIQ4 individuals have the wisdom to assess people and environments accurately, recognizing when to be assertive, motivational, analytical, or lighthearted. They can shift styles from one instant to the next, depending on what's needed in the conversation or the group dynamic.

The Chameleon dares to act on that understanding, even when it is uncomfortable. They don't allow the fear of judgment or rejection to sway them. Instead, their decisions are grounded in integrity; they choose to do what is right rather than what is easy or socially accepted. The Chameleon demonstrates an unwavering commitment to the truth of the moment, honoring their values and the well-being of others.

Those at Level 4 masterfully balance the dichotomies of their strengths and challenges. PIQ4 Eagles are both candid and tactful. Parrots radiate optimism while simultaneously being rooted in practicality. Doves can be generous without overextending themselves. Owls can seek quality outcomes without getting stuck on minor details.

Being around someone with a Chameleon-like presence feels easy and safe. Since they understand all four styles, they can make anyone feel understood and seen by meeting them where they are.

Maintain Authenticity

One way to become a Chameleon is to act as if you are one. In other words, read the style of the person you are interacting with and reflect it back to them. You are more likely to get what you want when those around you get what they want.

When I work with salespeople, I tell them, "If you are selling to someone whose style differs from yours, one of you will leave that interaction exhausted. And it better be you."

It requires extra effort to express a style different from your own, but the more you practice, the more natural it becomes.

Mirroring someone's style helps build rapport and strengthens the connection, ultimately leading to better results and conserving energy over time.

This is typically when someone raises a hand and asks if mirroring someone's style is manipulative. The answer is that it depends on your intention. If you adopt a different style to honor another person's needs, that's authentic. If you weaponize the styles to serve yourself at someone else's expense, that's manipulation.

Let's delve deeper into the concepts of manipulation and authenticity.

Merriam-Webster defines *manipulate* as "to control or play upon by artful, unfair, or insidious means especially to one's own advantage."

Manipulation is done for personal gain. It involves deceptive tactics and emotional exploitation aimed at shaping the thoughts, feelings, or actions of others without their awareness or consent.

Authenticity is on the other side of the coin. Merriam-Webster defines authenticity as being "true to one's personality, spirit, or character." It's about living in accordance with your genuine thoughts, emotions, and values. It means being true to yourself, embracing your unique traits, and not putting on a facade to conform to external expectations. Authentic individuals are comfortable with their imperfections and being vulnerable. They live their lives according to their principles and beliefs rather than those of others. Authentic people are not defined by external validation; they seek self-validation, defining success and happiness on their terms.

Sometimes, specific settings or roles require us to adapt our style to succeed. You may act one way at work but another when interacting with your children. That does not mean you lack authenticity. It simply means you can read a person or environment and act accordingly. If you treated your coworkers like your kids, it wouldn't go well.

Adaptability isn't about being two-faced or being someone you're not. It's the skill of tapping into a part of you that resonates with that part of them. Remember, we have all four brain quadrants, and thus, we all have the four styles within us.

When actors play a role, they are not pretending to be a character. They are reaching inward and drawing out the parts of themselves that align with the character. It's not about becoming someone else but about expressing a different facet of who they already are. When a Parrot shares extensive details with an Owl, they are not pretending to be an Owl. They are activating their inner Owl.

When we flex our styles to support people, we honor who they are. Speaking the local language in a foreign country is considered respectful, not manipulative. The same is true when we speak the language of another style, and those at Level 4 can speak the language of anyone they meet.

Since each style has different tendencies, each has specific challenges when it comes to maintaining authenticity. For Eagles, the pressure to maintain a dominant and authoritative image might lead them to suppress vulnerability or avoid admitting mistakes. Eagles may need to recognize that authenticity involves acknowledging their weaknesses. Expressing vulnerability can enhance trust and authenticity in their relationships.

Parrots may struggle with authenticity when it collides with their craving for approval and recognition. They have an intense longing for the love and admiration of others, even strangers, but what if their true thoughts and feelings are likely to be unpopular? Embracing authenticity involves staying true to oneself, even in the face of potential disapproval.

Doves may find it challenging to assert themselves authentically, especially during disagreements. Their strong preference for harmony might lead them to avoid confrontation or suppress their genuine opinions. Doves have to practice being assertive without feeling like they are being aggressive.

Owls may struggle with perfectionism and the fear of making mistakes. This can make them reluctant to take risks or share unfinished work and hinder authentic self-expression. They may need to recognize that authenticity includes embracing imperfections. Sharing the process of learning and growing, along with successes and failures, contributes to a more authentic and relatable persona.

Those who have attained the Chameleon state are authentic in everything they do. They have embraced all the styles. So, when they act, it is genuine.

Don't Impose Your Style on Others

We tend to believe that people want what we want and need what we need. As a result, we might impose our desires on others, assuming they will be fulfilled if we treat them how we want to be treated. As George Carlin observed, "Anybody driving slower than you is an idiot, and anyone going faster than you is a maniac." We think, whether consciously or unconsciously, *I'm pretty sure there is a right way, and I'm doing it.*

It's easy to get trapped in this assumption. After all, we have a lifetime of data indicating our way works. To be the Chameleon, we must let go of the belief that our style's way is the best and only way. We must embrace the idea that every style is valuable and necessary.

As a Parrot, instead of expecting your Dove child to be outgoing and highly social, honor their longing for quiet time and create a peaceful space for them to be themselves.

Likewise, if a friend prefers quiet, intimate gatherings over large parties, consider their preference when planning group events. In the workplace, instead of assuming a colleague prefers the same type of recognition you do, ask them how they like to be acknowledged for their contributions. And when dealing with customers, tailor your approach to each customer rather than applying a catch-all solution.

Level 4 of Personality Intelligence is built on unconditional acceptance of others. When we stop trying to change people and start honoring who they are, we bring out the best in them.

Identify the Styles of Others

To effectively adapt as a Chameleon, you must first be able to identify the styles of those around you. The first step in developing people-reading skills, or Bird Watching, as I call it, is to practice identifying the styles of everyone you meet. When I speak at events, I often suggest a homework assignment: go home, watch television or read a novel, and while you are doing so, focus on recognizing the styles of the characters you see. You can practice this skill anywhere—at work, out shopping, or any place you observe people. Like any skill, the more you practice, the better you become.

I introduced my children to the styles when they were six, and they quickly learned to recognize them in others. We'd be at a restaurant, and within seconds of the server taking our drink order, they'd say, "She's an Eagle" or "He's an Owl." If six-year-olds can do it, you can, too.

When figuring out someone's style, tune into their words, tone, and facial expressions. Relationship-oriented Doves and Parrots speak from the heart and often use "I feel" statements. Task-focused Owls and Eagles tend to say, "I think."

Pay attention to their posture, body language, and how they move. Do they convey Eagle self-confidence, Parrot excitement, Dove warmth, or Owl curiosity?

Notice that Eagles speak assuredly and maintain steady eye contact. They talk in assertive sound bites. Parrots have enormous energy, talk fast, and are highly animated. They tend to have a wide range of tone and body movements when speaking. Doves tend to move with intention and have gentler, slower movements. Their tone is softer and reassuring. Owl body language can be more formal and business-like. They may not convey much emotion in their facial expressions, which can make it harder to figure out how they are feeling or what they are thinking.

Look carefully at faces. Deep frown lines suggest the person worries a lot and may be an overthinking Owl. Parrots who smile and laugh often have crow's feet, the smile lines of joy.

Someone's smile can also tell you a lot about them. Parrots often have a big, toothy grin, while Doves have a gentle smile and may not show their teeth. Doves also tend to lightly pull up the sides of their lips, which creates endearing dimples. Owls often keep their lips together, even while smiling or laughing. Eagles typically have a closed-lip smile with their chin raised slightly and eyes that convey intensity.

Here's a two-question formula that will quickly help you identify someone's primary style:

Question One: Are they more outgoing or reserved? You are probably dealing with an Owl or Dove if they're more reserved. If they're outgoing, you have an Eagle or Parrot.

Question Two: Are they more concerned about people and feelings or facts and goals? They are likely to be a Parrot or Dove if they are more relationship-oriented. If they are more interested in tangible things like data or information, they are probably an Eagle or Owl. So, for example, a reserved, people-oriented person is a Dove, and an outgoing, goal-oriented person is an Eagle.

Here are ten more questions you can ask yourself to help figure out someone's style:

1. Is their handshake gentle or firm?

   Eagles tend to have strong handshakes while Doves are softer.

2. What do they mostly talk about?

   Eagles often talk about results, Parrots about themselves, Doves about relationships, and Owls about improving things.

3. How do they define success?

   For Eagles, success is winning; for Parrots, it's excitement; for Doves, it's everyone being happy; and for Owls, it's high-quality work.

4. How do they behave when in a position of authority?

   Eagles are authoritarian, Parrots are empowering, Doves are supportive, and Owls are process-oriented.

5. What kind of emails do they write?

   Eagle emails are brief with short sentences and strong language. If you encounter energy, exclamation points, and lots of emojis, you likely just got an email from a Parrot! Doves ask how you are doing and wish you well. Owls write detailed messages that often contain lots of questions.

6. Do they address how others will be affected by potential actions?

   This is a main concern for Doves.

7. How do they respond when things change?

Eagles adapt quickly, Parrots go with the flow, Doves may become uncomfortable, and Owls have a lot of questions.

8. How do they behave when driving?

Eagle impatience may cause them to drive aggressively; Parrots listen to music and enjoy the sights. Doves are considerate of other drivers; Owls are cautious.

9. How often do they take selfies?

Eagles and Owls rarely take selfies while Parrots take them often; Doves take pictures with other people. In fact, their social media avatar photo may include a significant other or their children.

10. How do they act when under the influence of alcohol?

This one's just for fun! Eagles tell people what to do; Parrots get funny; Doves listen deeply; and Owls get philosophical.

Match the Style to the Moment

In addition to reading people and adapting, sometimes we must assess the circumstances and adjust to what is required. Remember Cookie the gerbil? Isaac's Eagle coworker used the wrong style to comfort him. Regardless of the individual's style, some circumstances require Eagle, Parrot, Dove, or Owl mode. The Eagle may be ideal for closing a high-stakes business deal or making quick decisions in a crisis. The Parrot style may be just what is called for in a team-building activity or speech to a big, energetic audience. The Dove may be the perfect style to mediate conflict or validate an upset customer's concerns. The Owl may be perfectly suited for quality control or conducting in-depth research before making an important decision.

When considering how to adapt to a situation, pause and consider what style will create the optimal outcome. Using a simple mantra before reacting with preprogrammed responses can do the trick. Ask yourself, "What style is needed in this moment?" Then take a breath and see what arises. You might be surprised that you already know what to do. Just tap into your inner wisdom and listen.

Work on Your Low-Style Behaviors

To achieve PIQ4 status, an individual must master all four styles. This means developing the behaviors and skills that they display least often.

Look for opportunities to engage in the behaviors of your lowest style. The goal is to get comfortable and adept enough to exhibit them, even if it takes energy.

I remember watching Bill Gates in his younger days; he appeared nervous and awkward when being interviewed or speaking on stage. One notable example is a 1995 interview on the *Late Show* where he tries to explain the internet to a skeptical David Letterman. He was hunched over and tense through the shoulders, probably because fielding impromptu questions from a comedian with little knowledge of technology is stressful for an Owl.

But today, Gates seems comfortable and polished. Unlike Parrots, who might be excited in these settings, I imagine that he reached a neutral place where he doesn't get energized when being interviewed or speaking at conferences, but he's also not anxious. He developed his style to the point where he can do what must be done.

Enhancing your lower-style behaviors will enable you to become a Chameleon, giving you the ability to access any style, whenever it's needed.

The Chameleon Way

Every generation has stories of highly evolved individuals who captivate the human imagination. They seem to understand life's mysteries, offering wisdom that inspires personal transformation and collective progress. There is something special about these folks, and we often can't quite put our finger on it. But one thing is certain: We want to spend time with them.

Those at Level 4 tend to transcend mundane concerns and don't get caught up in drama. They know themselves deeply and accept people without judgment. They have learned to rise above egoic concerns and are committed to continuous learning. Despite their high level of development, true Chameleons exhibit humility. They acknowledge that there is always more to learn and recognize the contributions of those in their field. They often take on roles as mentors, teachers, or leaders as they model what we aspire to become. And, like Sensei Tori, they imbue every moment with opportunities to learn and grow closer to our highest self.

Level 4 in Action

In upcoming chapters, you will meet some real-life Chameleons. But before we get there, here's someone who has exemplified Level 4 adaptability for generations—a figure admired by children and adults around the world. Yes, I'm talking about the big guy himself, Santa Claus.

In Eagle mode, Santa is a master strategist with an ambitious annual goal of delivering toys to children worldwide in a single night. To do this, he must lead a highly complex operation at the North Pole. He manages a team of fun-loving elves and a herd of playful reindeer, which can't be easy. Santa's Owl side takes a methodical approach, classifying children as naughty or nice. And when it's time to organize his deliveries, he makes a list and checks it—not once, but twice! This extra attention to detail is pure Owl.

Santa's Parrot side fills the air with his signature hearty laugh and boundless exuberance. His charisma is magnetic, instantly lifting spirits and spreading holiday cheer wherever he goes.

And Santa's Dove qualities shine through in his gentle, attentive nature as he listens carefully to each child's holiday wishes, making them feel genuinely heard and valued. His mission to spread joy and give presents comes from a place of selfless generosity. Santa's dedication to making children feel loved is at the heart of the holiday spirit.

Santa's enduring legacy comes, in part, from his ability to embody all four styles. Santa Claus is truly the ultimate Chameleon.

Up Next

Now that you understand the four levels of Personality Intelligence, it is time to explore what each style looks like at each level. Get ready for some self-reflection!

Part III:
The Four Styles and Personality Intelligence

Chapter 9:
The Adventure Begins

Planning the Journey

During their first two decades at Sensei Tori's dojo, Dawn, Ian, Scarlett, and Carter became close friends. What began as a shared journey through the ranks became a bond that deepened with each new challenge they faced together.

Fifteen years ago, near the end of their senior year of high school, they went out for ice cream together. Ian expressed sadness that they would soon be heading in different directions after graduation. Scarlett proposed they take an annual vacation to stay connected. As they talked, the idea evolved into embarking on meaningful journeys that would push them to learn and grow. Carter pointed out that traveling every year might not be realistic, so they all agreed to travel every two years instead.

It was time to plan their next adventure, and the Zoom session was about to begin. Ian was excited to get the party started. "Greetings, fellow travelers!" he began.

"After all this time, you still have as much energy as the day I met you. I don't know how you do it," Scarlett said.

"I wake up smiling and go from there," Ian said, giggling to himself.

Dawn shook her head. "I believe him."

Carter was eager to get down to business. "I've been doing some research..."

"Of course, you have!" Ian interjected.

Carter continued without missing a beat. "As I was saying, I've been doing some research, and I think I have the perfect place."

"Just as long as it doesn't take as much time as the Camino de Santiago. Don't get me wrong, that was an impactful experience, but I can't take two weeks off from work," Dawn said.

"If it's okay with all of you, the European battlefield tour was too emotional for me. I can't handle another trip like that," Scarlett added.

"And that silent retreat at the Buddhist monastery nearly killed me," Ian joked.

"Don't worry, this one is only a weeklong, nobody died there, and you're allowed to talk," said Carter.

"Sounds great," Ian exclaimed. "Whaddya got for us?"

"That's what I'm trying to tell you. I found a place that, as Ian might say, will 'rock your world.' There are many details to share, but suffice it to say, we are going to engage in a deep exploration of ourselves."

"Can you give us a sense of what we would be doing?" Scarlett asked.

"For most of the week, we'll travel through Central Asia, visit ancient temples, take in the stunning mountain and river scenery, and do a bit of shopping in the local markets. Then, on the last day, we are going on the biggest exploration of all. We will be going on a vision quest and experiencing a unique spin on the sweat lodge tradition prevalent in cultures around the world. Did you know that in addition to the indigenous tribes in North, South, and Central America, people from Thailand, India, China, and Tibet all have sweat lodge traditions? But not only that, Ireland, Russia, Germany, and Finland too. I could keep going.

"I'm sure you could," Dawn said, attempting to move the conversation along.

"I'm in!" Ian declared.

"This sounds fascinating," Scarlett said.

"There are many facets to the experience. Dawn, since I know you like the bottom line, here it is: we'll each explore who we were, are, and could be. It might even help you be more successful at work."

"I feel like this is something we could all enjoy," Scarlett said.

"You had me at 'more successful.' Let's do it," Dawn nodded.

"But you don't have all the information yet," Carter cautioned.

"Don't need it. You did the research. You like it. That's good enough for me. Send us the info, and we'll book it. Everyone agree?" Dawn asked.

Everyone nodded.

"It will take a few days to gather all the details and logistics, but once I put it together, I will send it to you."

"Awesome!" Ian said. "You're the best. Thanks for doing the leg work. I appreciate you."

"Of course," replied Carter. "You can expect an email soon."

The Nest

After spending five days immersed in the sights and sounds of this magical land, the group set out on the final leg of their journey in a shuttle provided by as part of their excursion. They watched in awe as the scenery gradually transformed before their eyes. The bustling streets, alive with the hum of daily life, gradually gave way to rolling hills and winding roads.

Street vendors and storefronts were replaced by towering trees, their branches swaying gently in the mountain breeze. The rhythmic pulse of urban energy softened, merging with the tranquil sounds of nature—the rustling of leaves, the distant call of a bird, and the whisper of a cool wind weaving through the forest. The transition felt almost surreal, as if they were crossing into an entirely different world, one where time moved more slowly, and the air carried the earthy aroma of unfamiliar trees.

They pulled into a forest clearing where a woman, gray haired and serene, awaited them. Her smile, subtle and knowing, put the group at ease.

"Welcome. I am known as Dream Weaver. I hope you had a pleasant journey."

"A little bumpy at the end," Dawn replied, "but no worse for the wear."

"Wonderful. Everything is set up, so the only thing you need to bring are your focus objects. Does everyone have theirs?"

Everyone nodded as they wondered what the others had brought.

Dream Weaver gestured to a path through the woods. "Let us begin with open hearts and clear minds, for the journey is as vital as the destination."

She led the group through a deep canopy of willow trees and past spruce trees that stood watch over the landscape. The journey was long and winding, with the trail often disappearing among the trees. In the distance, they saw a domed structure assembled from branches. Outside the structure, referred to as the Nest, a man tended a pile of stones warming in a fire pit.

"Those rocks look mighty hot," Ian said, filling the silence.

With a gravelly voice that seemed to contain the wisdom of the ages, the man replied, "These are Memory Stones. They hold the power of the earth and will guide you on your way."

Dream Weaver introduced the man as her brother and called him the Fire Keeper. She led the group to the Nest's opening. Before they entered, the Fire Keeper placed the red-hot stones into the pit at the center of the Nest.

The group removed their shoes and stripped down to the bathing suits under their clothes, thus leaving behind the physical symbols of everyday life. Dream Weaver handed each of them a small branch adorned with leaves to use as a fan. Crouching low, the friends entered the Nest, feeling the earth's warmth beneath their feet. The space was dark, illuminated only by the glow of the Memory Stones.

Dream Weaver began the ceremony by pouring water over the heated rocks, releasing a cloud of steam that filled the Nest. She led a chant, calling on the spirits to purify and protect those within.

With each breath, the four visitors released the tension they had brought with them. They could feel the sweat beading on their skin.

Dream Weaver said, "The water I poured onto these stones is not ordinary water. This sacred flow of the planet has been infused with the leaves of a rare plant my forebears discovered long ago. The plant's name has never been written down, and its name cannot be spoken. Just know that you are safe in the embrace of those who have come before you.

"The aromatic scent of this plant can trigger key flashbacks that represent your true essence. As you breathe in, I will guide you to experience the tapestry that weaves your life's path. We will rewind time to reveal the true you. We will uncover moments that capture who you are today. Then, we will go on a vision quest to see where you can go if you follow the path of your spirit. Although you will each experience your own adventure, you will see as your friends see, hear as they hear, and dream as they dream. Though your paths may differ, the wind that whispers to one ear will carry the same message to another. Walk with open hearts and listening spirits, for the journey is not only yours—it is shared with those beside you. Respect their visions as you would honor your own."

Dream Weaver led an invocation to acknowledge their spiritual presence and seek blessings and then welcomed the group to chant and drum with her. The group relaxed and settled in as the scent of roots and berries filled the air. Dream Weaver asked who would like to go first.

"I'll go!" Ian proclaimed, rarely one to hesitate.

And so, it was.

Chapter 10:
The Parrot

The Level 1 Parrot

Dream Weaver faced Ian. "Today, we will explore the path of your spirit and the wisdom that lies within. I will help you navigate the landscapes of your inner world, where the past and present meet. We will sit with the times when you have walked in harmony with your true self and reflect on the times you have wandered from that path.

"These teachings that the wind whispers to us guide us to understand who we are and who we are meant to be. As we walk together, remember that every step, whether strong or faltering, is part of the sacred circle of life. In each place, we find a lesson, a memory, and a chance to grow closer to the essence of who we are.

"Before we begin, set your focus object before you. Since you have chosen an item that speaks to who you are, it will help guide your thoughts to shine your true inner light," Dream Weaver said.

Ian reached into his bag and removed three colorful, knitted hacky sack balls. His three companions burst into laughter.

"Are you still learning how to juggle?" Carter asked.

"Learning? More like learned! I can juggle for almost fifteen seconds."

"So, not quite fifteen seconds?" Carter clarified.

"I'm rounding up."

"Focus on these objects and let the grand events of your life drift away like leaves carried in the wind. Turn your gaze to the small, quiet times that often go unnoticed. Do not seek to summon a particular event, for the stories that genuinely hold your essence will arise on their own. I ask you to journey back through time, allowing these moments to come forth like a river revealing its hidden depths.

"Return to your earliest memory, where your spirit first began to awaken. What do you see, my child? Let these memories speak, for they carry the wisdom of your true self. Do not question or judge what arises."

Ian sat in stillness, patiently waiting for something to emerge. It didn't take long.

> Oooh, I see something! This is an odd sensation. It's like I'm watching myself, but I am also experiencing it. I feel like I am in both the past and present at the same time.

"Just be present and share that which is revealed," Dream Weaver said.

> Okay. I got this. I see myself. I'm young—maybe eight years old. I'm walking home from school holding a brown envelope. It's my report card, and I am not happy. My parents are *not* going to like my teachers' comments. It says, "Ian seems more interested in talking with his classmates than learning. I have moved his seat several times, but he continues to talk to whoever sits beside him."

"I see," Dream Weaver responded. "Is it true that you used to talk a lot?"

"It's still true!" answered Dawn.

"The more things change, the more they stay the same," added Carter.

"I never did win the Quiet Game," acknowledged Ian.

"Let's move on," suggested Dream Weaver. "Allow the sights and feelings to reveal themselves to you. Tell us what you see."

> Oh, I remember this day. I am about ten years old and climbing into my parents' pillows. And I mean that literally—the pillows are next to each other on the bed. I've just placed my legs into my father's pillow with the fluffy part on top of me.
>
> Now, I'm pulling my mother's pillow over the top half of my body, creating a cozy cocoon. They look like ordinary pillows from the outside, but I'm hiding inside.

Fast-forward about ten minutes. Right after my parents get into bed, I jolt upright with a loud yell. They both go into a frenzy of terror.

Good times, good times.

"Something tells me they didn't enjoy that as much as you did," Scarlett said.

"Something told you correctly," agreed Ian.

"I feel bad for your parents," whispered Scarlett, just loud enough for all to hear.

"You have no idea," Ian chuckled.

"Let us move forward to a new event in your life," suggested Dream Weaver. "Share what you see."

Here we go. I'm in my fifth-grade class. We are learning about the properties of various shapes. The teacher is explaining how a square is a type of rectangle because it has four sides with four right angles. She then asked if a rectangle is a type of a square. Of course, it is not, because a square requires all four sides to be equal length.

And yet, I raise my hand with dramatic flair and answer, "A rectangle *can* become a square—if it believes in itself." The class cracks up. Now that I think about it, the teacher made the same eye-rolling expression Carter often makes at the things I say.

"I admit that it's funny, but it's inappropriate in that setting," Carter said.

"We can agree to disagree on that one," countered Ian.

"Clearly, humor is part of your world," Dream Weaver concluded. "Let's move along. Advance forward in time. What do you see?"

The group fanned themselves with the leafy branches while Ian waited for a story to arise.

> Oh, this is classic. I'm eating dinner with my parents, and my birthday is approaching in a few weeks. My dad asks if there is anything special I would like to do on my birthday.
>
> "I'd like to have a big surprise party," I say.
>
> "Ummmm, you get the nature of a surprise party, right?" my dad says. He reminds me of Dawn sometimes.
>
> "Totally. I'll act surprised."
>
> Sure enough, it was the best day of my life up to that point.

"Ian as the center of attention? Shocking!" Carter joked.

Dawn turned to Dream Weaver. "If you're keeping track, Ian loves the spotlight."

"I sense that friends are a big part of your story," said Dreamweaver. "Let us journey to a time when you walked alongside them. Let your heart open to the memory of your friends. What do you see?"

Yet again, Ian grinned.

> I'm in my backyard, where my mom has been reminding me to clean up my toys and sporting equipment for days. She says my dad is planning to mow the lawn over the weekend, and too many things are scattered across the grass. Seven of my friends arrive. They want to play basketball at the nearby park, and I really want to join them.
>
> As if on cue, my mother looks through the kitchen window into the backyard and shakes her head in disbelief. My friends are cleaning up the yard!

"How did that come to pass," Dream Weaver asked.

> Well, I explained to my friends that since the game requires an even number of players, and that I can't join them until everything in my yard is put away, the best course of action is for them to help me clean up. They agree, and voila, I've hired free workers to straighten the yard!

"Ian can get anyone to do anything," Scarlett quietly said.

"Classic Ian," said Carter, as he shook his head.

"He used his powers of persuasion to manipulate. Am I the only one who sees this?" Dawn asked with amusement.

"He was developing his ability to be influential. It's quite impressive," Scarlett replied.

"I can see that you have strong communication skills. How about another experience from when you were in school?" asked Dream Weaver.

Ian sat silently, then winced.

> I'm standing on a stage at school, but I must admit, my star is not shining brightly. For weeks, I told my friends that I was learning how to juggle. I am proud of my progress and got to the point where I can juggle three balls for five to ten seconds. I figure that's pretty good for a twelve-year-old. But I maaaaay have exaggerated the extent of my juggling ability.
>
> As luck would have it, the fifth-grade class is putting on a school play with a circus theme. One of my friends suggests that I juggle in the show. The teacher asks me if I can juggle. My friends are there, and I feel like I have no choice but to say, "Yes."

Ian paused, hoping he wouldn't have to relive the rest.

"How did it go?" asked Dream Weaver.

"Let's just say I dropped the ball."

"*You* exaggerate your skills?!," said Dawn, laughing at her friend's predictability.

Scarlett's face showed a look of sympathy.

"I remember telling myself not to embellish the story," Ian said, sullenly. "Every now and then, I have to relearn that one."

"Sometimes, learning is uncomfortable," Dream Weaver said. "And that is why you are here. To uncover the patterns of the past so that you don't repeat your failures. I must commend your vulnerability for letting us into the shadows.

"Now, journey a bit further along the path of time. Perhaps you find yourself at college. Share what you see in this new chapter."

It's near the end of my first semester of freshman year. I have a fifteen-page paper due on Monday. It's Friday, and I have barely started working on it. I was going to do it the previous weekend, but my friends were going hiking, and I wanted to go. So, I did.

Unfortunately for me, the professor wants us to use a lot of sources, which I definitely did not do. Instead, I use my imagination to write a story that beautifully captures the topic. When he reads it, he says that if he could award an A for creativity, my paper would be the best in the class, but I didn't follow directions. I just didn't have the time. I get a D+ and it really stings.

"You prioritized pleasure over work?" Dream Weaver asked.

"Yeah, I did that a lot back then. I still do that today, but not as much."

"Let's visit one more of your life stories. Speak of what comes to you," Dream Weaver said.

This is an interesting one. My friend's home has burned to the ground, and I feel so bad for her. She is so sad, and I want to be helpful. I think I can lift her spirits by sharing the positive side of this terrible event, so, I comment on her social media post, "On the bright side, think about how exciting it will be to get all new stuff."

Let's just say that elicits many comments suggesting that I should be more sensitive. I would handle that very differently now.

"Sounds like you've had some learning," Dream Weaver said.

"Definitely," replied Ian.

"Let us pause to re-center ourselves and allow the Fire Keeper to tend to the stones. We shall reconvene soon."

Reflections on the Level 1 Parrot

When Ian begins his journey, we see him in his early childhood. These stories embody the Parrot at the first level of Personality Intelligence. It's important to note that while these examples are of the Parrot as a child and young adult, anyone at any age can display Level 1 behaviors.

When we first meet young Ian, we discover his talkativeness in the classroom. Parrots tend to fill silence with words or activity. They may even cut people off mid-story when they have something exciting to share. By taking up all the airtime in a conversation, the Level 1 Parrot can make others feel uncared for and unheard.

At PIQ1, Parrot humor can come at the expense of those around them. There's nothing wrong with having fun, and in the case of the pillow prank, he had no harmful intentions. Of course, I'm saying this as a reformed Parrot prankster (okay, *mostly* reformed). Parrots at this level can cause unintentional harm because they don't consider how their prank or joke will affect others. They come up with an idea and act without thinking things through.

Parrots at this stage don't have a finely tuned filter that tells them when to share their humorous thoughts and when to hold them back. When Ian raised his hand in class to say something funny; he added some levity, but it might not have been the right time, as it disrupted the lesson. PIQ1 Parrots lack the impulse control to hold thoughts that may be better left unsaid or said at a more appropriate time.

They also have an insatiable craving for attention and validation. Parrots revel in the spotlight, which is why Ian lobbied for a surprise party to celebrate his birthday. They fear fading into the background and must be witnessed in everything they do. We've all met the child who constantly says, "Watch this!" or "Look what I did!" They crave to be seen. And if you don't witness them with delighted exuberance, they may feel you disapprove of what they have done or created. So, they might try something even more spectacular to get that attention.

From there, we watched Ian convince his friends to clean his backyard. Highly evolved Parrots can be incredibly persuasive. That's one of the reasons more salespeople are Parrots than any other style. However, persuasion can devolve into manipulation at the Unevolved State. While asking friends for assistance is okay, Ian just didn't feel like doing his chores, so he foisted them on others using manipulative logic.

Then, when Ian embellished his juggling abilities, he displayed a behavior typical of Level 1 Parrots. As natural storytellers, Parrots want to captivate others with their stories and with their abilities. That's a recipe for exaggeration. As they evolve, Parrots learn to tell stories without needing an Owl to correct the details.

With a strong desire to enjoy life, pleasure precedes everything else for Parrots at this stage. Notice how Ian prioritized fun with friends over an assignment in college. PIQ1 Parrots might resent having responsibilities and neglect them as a result. Even adult Parrots might go to a movie they've wanted to see instead of grocery shopping, cleaning the house, or completing their taxes. That can create avoidable chaos and stress, for themselves and others.

In this initial growth stage, Parrots are repelled by pessimism and complaints. They try to reframe anything negative in a positive light, such as when Ian's friend lost her home to a fire. That way, they avoid having to deal with a difficult issue and stay in fun mode.

Each style can tend to take responsibility for things that are not theirs to own. Parrots may feel the overwhelming need to lighten things up when life gets heavy. Imagine a Parrot in a staff meeting; the conversation is intense and they interject with a funny joke. It may fall like a lead balloon, as their humor doesn't match the gravity of the situation. At this first stage, Parrots may take ownership of boosting morale or ensuring everyone is having fun; however, this may not be their role, or it may just be inappropriate—and it may cause them to gloss over the real issues.

The Level 2 Parrot

In the heart of the Nest, the Fire Keeper tended to the Memory Stones. With a reverent touch, he poured his sacred water over the rocks, and steam filled the Nest.

"Let's continue on your path," said Dream Weaver to Ian. "Your journey through life has allowed your true essence to begin to shine. Let us move to the next event your spirit wishes to reveal."

"If it's okay," Scarlett said, "I feel moved to share what happened on the first day of our college orientation."

"That would be wonderful. Sometimes, the magic of this place works through others. If you are being called to share a story, it must be important."

"I was sitting in the basketball arena for freshman orientation. Ian was a member of the team that was running the event. Everyone was sitting quietly, which makes sense, since we didn't know anyone.

"Ian came to our section and told us to turn to the person next to us, introduce ourselves, and share a little about ourselves. Well, that got many of us talking, but that wasn't enough for Ian. Next thing I knew, he grabbed the microphone and told thousands of people to introduce themselves to their neighbors."

"Ian, what prompted you to do that?" Dream Weaver asked.

"When we came in, the place was lifeless. There was no music and no excitement. Can you imagine how it felt to be in a silent arena? I wanted to change the energy and started going section by section to get everyone talking. But I quickly realized that the arena was too big for me to get to everyone. So, I took the mic and made it happen."

"It was incredible how he changed the feeling of the place. I'd seen him do this in karate class, but this was next level," Scarlett said proudly.

"That reminds me of a different Ian story. Would you mind if I share it?" Carter asked.

"Have at it!" said Ian.

"A few years back, Ian and I spent a few days in Las Vegas. After we checked in for our flight home, there was a four-hour flight delay. Our flight was eventually canceled and there wasn't another one until the next day.

"I was frustrated that we were stuck when we had to return to our lives. But not Ian. He was like, 'Bonus vacation day!' Within minutes, he went online and got us a suite at one of the resorts on the Strip for 75 percent off. Then, we had a great dinner, got cheap tickets to see a show, and flew home the next day. He always finds a way to turn lemons into lemonade."

"That's a tremendous skill," said Dream Weaver. "Let's all let that sink in and Ian, when you're ready—"

"Oh, I've got plenty more!"

"Indeed, you do," said Dream Weaver, "and we shall join you for them. Inhale deeply and let the air you breathe lift your spirit beyond the Earth realm."

My son and I are standing in line at a fast-food restaurant. The person behind the counter looks both young and inexperienced. I sense he just started working there and this is his first job.

After serving the customers ahead of us, he is returning to the register and bumps into the manager. Inexplicably, she loudly yells at her new employee, telling him that if he can't focus, maybe he shouldn't be working here.

The restaurant grows quiet, and the poor guy looks flustered. I can't help myself. When it's my turn to order, I tell him, in what might be a voice loud enough for the manager and everyone else in the restaurant to hear, "Look, bumping into your manager was a mistake. We are all human. We all make mistakes. But what she did, correcting you in front of everyone here, is inappropriate. When you go home today, don't think you did anything wrong. She was the one who did something wrong."

At that point, the manager turns to *me* and says firmly, "Sir, this is not your concern."

I look back at the kid. "And now, she's yelling at the customer."

She storms off.

I just couldn't let that sit. It wasn't right of her to yell at him. And I didn't want him to feel bad, or even worse, let a poor manager damage his self-esteem. I had to say something.

"Well, you earned some good karma points that day, my friend," Scarlett said.

"Nicely done, Ian," Dream Weaver said. "It sounds like injustice is something that upsets you. Take a minute to breathe before continuing."

Ian flinched and began.

> This happened at work. As the sales manager, I want to celebrate the success of one of my team members. At this point, she's been with us for twenty years, and in the past year, she made more sales than any salesperson in our company's history. I want to celebrate that and her twentieth anniversary, so, I hatch a plan. I hire a videographer to visit several of her clients to capture what makes her so special. We also collect comments from our employees. It's an amazing video.
>
> When we dim the lights, I bring her onstage, put a spotlight on her, and show the film. She becomes extremely uncomfortable, to say the least. Afterward, she says to me, "If you ever do something like that again, you won't have to worry about me anymore, because I won't be working here." In retrospect, I hadn't considered that she was fairly shy.

"Yikes," Dawn said. "The last thing you want to do is lose your number one salesperson."

"You can say that again. I thought she would love it. People said wonderful things about her. How could she not? I would have been riding high for days."

"That would have made me squirm," Scarlett said.

"I know that now!" replied Ian.

"What a wonderful learning opportunity. The Great Spirit is leading you to the threads that weave the tapestry of your life. Sit in your quiet space and see what wishes to be seen," Dream Weaver said.

Ian immediately began sharing his next experience.

> I am preparing for a game-changing sales call with a potential client and I'm nervous with anticipation. Before the meeting, I have to gather information from people throughout my organization. I don't sense any urgency, so I give them what I think is an energizing pep talk, conveying how big and important this sale will be for our company. I explain how this client can change the trajectory of our company.
>
> Evidently, I was a bit too enthusiastic because I freak everyone out. I just wanted to make sure they felt the same sense of urgency that I did.
>
> Throughout the next few days, I feel better after seeing a flurry of activity. I am ecstatic when I finally close the deal, but everyone else seems more relieved than

excited. Looking back, I realize I may have caused unnecessary drama.

"I'm the exact opposite," shared Carter. I'd get nervous if I saw everyone running around like chickens with their heads cut off. I'd prefer if they were calm and focused."

"It's beautiful when we celebrate our differences. Thank you for sharing that, Carter," Dream Weaver said.

"Where are we going now, Ian?" asked Dream Weaver.

I must admit, I'm kind of proud of this. My organization is about to implement a new Enterprise Resource Planning system—it's a fancy name for something that integrates finance, HR, supply chain, etc. into one system—and I'm in charge of making it happen. To make this even more complicated, the last time we made a major process change, there was so much resistance that we ultimately abandoned it. And this was waaaay bigger, so I am committed to fixing the problems we had last time.

Somewhere along the line, I learned that people support what they help to create, so, I lead several town hall events to keep everyone informed and ask them what they want. I also lead many meetings to answer questions and keep everyone informed.

We had some bumps in the road, but they are technical, not emotional. When we are ready, I coordinate a fun kickoff event. Then, after it is up and running, I organize a party to celebrate our success. And when I honor individual contributions, I make sure not to put anyone on the spot. I don't want to embarrass anyone."

"See how each of your previous steps make your next ones more grounded and stable," noted Dream Weaver. "Let's pause here. I sense that the Fire Keeper wants to tend to the stones. After that, we will project forward to the future."

Reflections on the Level 2 Parrot

At Level 2 of Personality Intelligence, there are times when people shine and other times when the challenges of their style create darker outcomes. The good times reflect skills developed along the way through trial and error. These new abilities help cultivate strong relationships and professional success. Conversely, the shadow times harken back to Level 1 behaviors and can create stress or conflict. At PIQ2, one may still exhibit some behaviors associated with PIQ1, though they may not be as extreme or damaging.

As Ian grew, we saw his style begin to shine. However, some of the challenges he faced in his youth remain. Remember, Level 2 is the Typical State where we have strengths and challenges.

On one hand, Parrots can generate excitement, like Ian getting the crowd talking during college orientation. It's a good bet that if you're a Parrot like Ian, you communicate with positivity, animating your words with various inflections, tones, and body language. This may enable you to motivate and inspire people. On the other hand, it's likely that if you are a Parrot, you have a strong dislike for silence that may get you into trouble. As President Calvin Coolidge once said, "Nobody ever listened themselves out of a job."

Parrots dislike silence and will go to great lengths to fill it! If you watch a Parrot eating dinner with someone of a different style and calculate the percentage of time the Parrot speaks versus their companion, it's a good bet that the Parrot will talk the most. Some indigenous cultures believe that each person is given a certain number of words to speak in their lifetime and once you use them up, your life ends. Parrots, I have bad news for you.

The inverse of speaking is listening. While listening, Parrots run the search engine inside their brain. As you share a story about your dog, they search for their own funny stories about dogs. Once they find one, they can think of nothing but sharing that story. And if you take too long, you can almost see them vibrating with the urge to speak. If you pause to inhale a breath, they may jump in with their story. At PIQ1 and PIQ2, Parrots listen to respond.

When encountering challenges, like the canceled flight out of Las Vegas, Parrots find the silver lining and make the best of whatever happens. Negativity, pessimism, and naysaying are intolerable to the Parrot, so they reframe it without even trying. When a Parrot must convey something negative, they take a positive word and negate it. For example, a Parrot would never say, "This is bad." Instead, they would say, "This is not good" or "I was not happy."

Recently, a friend of mine was dealing with poison ivy. I tried to empathize with her and expressed how uncomfortable she must be. She replied, "It's not the most fun I've ever had." For the Parrot, even poison ivy is on the fun scale. It's just down at the low end.

When Ian encountered an individual being treated disrespectfully by his manager at the fast-food restaurant, he instinctively commented on it. While Parrots tend to dislike conflict, they are repelled by disrespect. If they see someone being treated unfairly or improperly, they might insert themselves, even if they don't know the person. When they see disagreements, they might seek to diffuse the situation with humor. Sometimes, this works; other times, this can prevent the conflict from being resolved.

We saw three instances of Ian in the workplace. In the first, Ian tried to celebrate someone's accomplishments. This person was likely a Dove who didn't like the spotlight. While he sought to recognize the contributions of a valued team member, he also failed to demonstrate Personality Intelligence by neglecting to recognize and honor her style. He imposed his Parrot style on her, thinking she would like what he likes.

In the next workplace scenario, we watched Ian dealing with a stressful time as he prepares for an important sales presentation. When Parrots are stressed, everyone around them knows it! Recall Iago, the colorful parrot in Disney's *Aladdin*, who frustratedly proclaims, "Look at this. Look at this. I'm so ticked off that I'm molting!" Yeah, it's like that.

Parrots feel a sense of release in sharing their stress with others. It makes them feel better, but they might unwittingly stress out those around them. Ian externalized his stress, and people in the organization took it in. You won't need to figure out if a Parrot is stressed. You will know it because they will tell you, repeatedly.

In the third work story, Ian implemented large-scale organizational change. He learned from previous experiences and used his Parrot abilities to generate buy-in and support for the new process. This is one of the talents of the Parrot style, and Ian has developed this ability as a leader.

Parrot leaders at PIQ2 can be charismatic and inspirational. If they focus on the innate abilities of their style, they create a lively and enjoyable environment where morale is high. They may even describe the workplace culture they developed as their organization's secret sauce.

The Level 3 Parrot

Following a short break, everyone settled into the Nest.

"It is time to look forward to the path before you," Dream Weaver began. "We have reached the point in your journey where you can continue to step into the full essence of your being by embracing the vast universal polarities.

"Those who came before us spoke of the Great Balance. Just as day is followed by night and summer by winter, life is a dance between opposites. To walk this path is to embrace this balance, understanding that within every victory, there is humility, and within every weakness, there is a complementary strength.

"Ian, with the help of your friends, we are going to explore the opposites that, once brought into balance, will take you to places you couldn't have imagined. Close your eyes." Gesturing to the others, Dream Weaver said, "I want you each to share one of Ian's innate qualities. What makes Ian special?"

"I have always been impressed by his optimism," Dawn shared. "He finds the bright side in everything."

"Beautiful," acknowledged Dream Weaver. "Now, let us bring that into balance. What could he use to create balance?"

"Realism," Carter replied.

"Yes," confirmed Dream Weaver. "In the highest expression of Ian's spirit, he upholds his positive spirit while grounding it with reality."

"I've always been impressed by how Ian lives in the moment," Carter added.

"The most enlightened individuals embrace the present, but there is always an opposite. How does that work against you?" Dream Weaver asked Ian.

"Sometimes, I sacrifice my responsibilities to have fun. I get so caught up in what's happening that I forget to take care of what needs to be done. I have to find a balance between enjoying the present and handling my responsibilities."

"Wonderful, let's keep going. What's another one of Ian's gifts?"

"Ian is a great communicator. He always seems to know what to say and how to say it," Scarlett added.

"Ian, what's the flip side of that?" asked Dream Weaver.

"I suppose I talk more than I listen."

"Ahhhh, you must find harmony between the words you speak and the silence between them."

"That will be difficult," said Ian. "But I can see how that will help me."

"You often share the things that are going well in your life," Carter added.

"I'm sensing there's a but...," Ian smirked.

"You don't always share the bad things in your life. It sometimes makes me feel like my life is boring or more challenging than yours."

"Wow, I've never thought about it that way. I will work on that."

"May I share another?" Scarlett asked quietly.

"Of course," nodded Dream Weaver.

"I have always been impressed by how Ian is comfortable in the spotlight."

"If I'm beginning to understand the pattern," said Ian, "I also have to do a better job at letting others share their light instead of living in the shadow of my stories."

"Yes!" affirmed Dream Weaver. "The path is opening before you."

"You are incredible at making intuitive, gut-based decisions," Carter said, as if he'd reviewed many of those decisions first. "To create balance, I suggest adding data to your decision-making process."

"I would agree with that," Ian replied. "In that same light, I sometimes share my vision for the future with my team, but I don't provide much detail. I can see how sharing specifics would create more balance as well."

"Ian's charisma is truly magnetic," said Dawn. "However, I'd suggest incorporating a bit of seriousness on occasion. It might generate greater respect."

"Ian, before we close out your portion of this day, do you have any more you would like to add?" Dream Weaver asked.

"I've been listening, which I probably need to do more of."

The group's laughter confirmed that beyond doubt.

"I would add that balancing spontaneity with planning would probably serve me well. Winging it doesn't always yield the most positive results."

"The world is woven with threads of opposites—light and shadow, gentle and firm, talking and listening," Dream Weaver said with a wink at Ian. "To walk a harmonious path, you must learn to bring these forces into balance. In this way, you honor the harmony of the Great Spirit and walk the distance on your own path.

"I believe the Fire Keeper wants to tend to our Memory Stones. Let us give him the space to do so."

Reflections on the Level 3 Parrot

Individuals express their best selves at Level 3. Just as yin balances yang, those at PIQ3 balance the polarities of their style. They capitalize on their strengths but don't overuse them. They tap into the opposite of their traits to create balance.

Recall that in William Marston's model, Parrots perceive themselves as more powerful than the world and view the world as a friendly place. With that mindset, life is good. If they face challenges, they believe they can overcome them. If they need help, they believe they will be supported. This is the birthplace of Parrot optimism and conveys what Parrots must learn to master their style.

Studies repeatedly show that the most optimistic people tend to be happy, healthier, more successful at school and at work, and that they have relatively less stress and even live longer. But if the Parrot pushes this too far, it keeps them from attaining their highest level of being. They need to bring their positive outlook into balance.

At Level 3, Parrots see the bright side while considering potential challenges or risks. They envision an exciting future and consider the essential details that must be addressed. They hold realistic expectations for themselves and everyone else as they anticipate positive outcomes while addressing potential risks. Mastering optimism is central to the Parrot's evolution.

PIQ3 Parrots express the full range of their style's strengths while staying grounded by balancing them with the qualities of their opposite. This elevates them to the highest level of Personality Intelligence within their style.

Real-Life Level 3 Parrots

I'd like to paint a picture of style mastery in today's world with real people. I have chosen people who demonstrate a more profound mastery of their dominant style than most. For these individuals, I believe that it is not just their talent but also their highly evolved style that has led to their success.

Lady Gaga

Beyond Lady Gaga's incredible voice and artful performances, her vibrant Parrot charisma has helped her attain a level of popularity that few performers achieve. Like a Parrot who enjoys variety and spontaneity, Lady Gaga fluidly navigates various musical genres—from pop and rock to jazz and country. Albums like *Chromatica* showcase her energetic and playful approach to music, filled with catchy hooks and danceable beats that resonate with her audience.

Her willingness to collaborate with a diverse range of artists across genres, from Ariana Grande to Elton John to Tony Bennett, reflects her outgoing nature and drive for creative connections.

On stage, Lady Gaga is known for her high-energy performances that often incorporate elaborate choreography, theatrical elements, and visually stunning costumes. In her 2017 Super Bowl halftime show, Gaga opened with a calm "God Bless America" and "This Land Is Your Land" before literally diving off the rooftop of Houston's NRG Stadium (in a harness). She landed on a tower where she sang "Poker Face" with fireworks shooting off in the background. As if that weren't enough, Gaga closed the show with "Bad Romance" choreographed to an array of flamethrower towers. Parrot at the highest level.

Offstage, Lady Gaga actively engages with her fans on social media, sharing personal stories, insights into her life, and behind-the-scenes content. She also uses her Parrot style to promote important social issues, often with an upbeat approach. Her advocacy for mental health and LGBTQ+ rights is infused with hope, positivity, and a clear mission. Gaga says she speaks openly about using mental health medications to erase the stigma and judgment around them.

Look no further than her outrageous fashion choices to see her colorful Parrot style in action. Let's face it, an Owl would not wear a provocative meat dress to an awards show as Gaga did at the 2010 MTV Video Music Awards.

But as you just learned, those at PIQ3 balance their style with its complement. Lady Gaga balances her Parrot with the thoughtful Owl. Her writing in songs like "Million Reasons" shows her ability to explore complex emotions and themes. Her music videos showcase the Owl's love for detail and intellectual engagement, creating layered, conceptual performances that resonate on multiple levels. People continue to debate what Lady Gaga is communicating through the images and storyline of sex trafficking in her "Bad Romance" music video.

Between all the glamorous selfies on Instagram, Lady Gaga also taps into her inner Owl. In one post, she shares her favorite excerpts from *In Pursuit of Revolutionary Love*, a dense, challenging book by political theorist Joy James. She highlights and captions the text the way an Owl reading for a class might.

While Lady Gaga's eclectic Parrot style has propelled her to success, her thoughtful Owl has kept her grounded.

Michael Strahan

Being a superstar football player and a Parrot doesn't guarantee success as a television personality. Outgoing people struggle to hold an audience's attention day after day. But former defensive end Michael Strahan, a Super Bowl champion with the 2007 New York Giants, made the switch. His TV career has soared into outer space—quite literally.

As a player, Strahan's Parrot superpower was to relieve tension and uplift his teammates. Known for toothy smiles, jokes, and jabs, he seemed to preserve the fun and playfulness of football for his teammates and opponents.

At Super Bowl XLII, Strahan amped up his defensive line with a Parrot pep talk on the sidelines, saying: "17–14 is the final, okay? 17–14 fellas. One touchdown and we are world champions. Believe it, and it will happen." Sure enough, the Giants scored a last-minute touchdown to beat the Patriots 17-14.

That Super Bowl took Owl-like preparation. Strahan was known to spend hours in the film room studying his opponents. He studied each quarterback and knew their favorite plays under pressure and their release times. He set the record for sacks with 22.5 in the 2001 season. It takes immense discipline and preparation to read professional quarterbacks that well.

In his TV career as an NFL analyst and talk show host, Strahan continued to balance Parrot performance with Owl preparation. On *Live! with Kelly and Michael*, Strahan always burst onto the set with his trademark energy, waving and smiling as if he were greeting old friends. And he wasn't shy about sharing his goofy side. In an infamous Halloween episode, Strahan dressed up as Lando Calrissian from *Star Wars*, Cookie Lyon from the TV show *Empire*, and "Crazy Eyes" from *Orange is the New Black* among others.

On *Good Morning America*, it was clear that Strahan spent countless hours reviewing scripts, developing talking points, and preparing for interviews. He figured out how to guide interviewees into meaningful and sometimes difficult conversations. Some hosts sound like they've barely read the bullet points about each guest, but Strahan is always well-prepared; it feels like he's read their entire life story.

That's what a Level 3 Parrot can do when they've harmonized their warmth and enthusiasm with the Owl's attention to detail. No wonder Jeff Bezos invited Strahan to join his space travel company, Blue Origin, for its third adventure into suborbital space as an honorary guest. Strahan may not have any personal or professional attachment to space travel, but you know he prepared diligently, followed safety protocols, and made the public feel like they weren't just witnesses to the action, but part of the journey when he later shared about his experience.

Strahan's Parrot charisma and Owl preparation are serving him well in his career.

Chapter 11:
The Eagle

The Level 1 Eagle

The group returned to the Nest, and Dream Weaver resumed the ceremony. "Who would like to go next?"

"I will," declared Dawn.

Scarlett smiled quietly, enjoying her old friend's go get 'em attitude.

Dawn reached into her pack and removed a shiny gold karate trophy. Everyone's jaws dropped.

"What, pray tell, is that?" Ian asked.

"Uhhhh, I think it's obvious. It's a trophy from a karate tournament."

"But we didn't go to tournaments," Carter said, puzzled.

"Well, I did. I wanted to test my skills and guess what? I won."

Scarlett shook her head as if to say, *Only Dawn would do this.*

Dream Weaver pulled the group together and guided Dawn to focus on what her object represents to her.

"Let's go back in time to an instance that captures the true essence of your spirit. Tell us what you see."

Without hesitating, Dawn said, "This is strange. I feel like I'm watching a movie of myself, but I am also experiencing it."

"Just allow the images to come through. Do not judge or evaluate them. You will have time for that later," Dream Weaver advised.

Dawn drew a long breath.

> It's an odd sensation, but I'll roll with it. I am young, just four years old. We just got a dog, a puppy. My parents name her Marcette, but I don't like that. The dog is a collie, and I like the TV show with Lassie, who happens to be a collie. I decide that our dog's name is Lassie. They try to get me to call her Marcette, but I refuse.
>
> My parents don't want to confuse the dog and I refuse to back down. So, Lassie it is.

"That sounds on-brand," said Carter. "You always know what you want."

"Let's continue," Dream Weaver insisted. "What is your spirit speaking to you now?"

> Something is coming through. I'm still young, five or six. I'm playing cards with my grandmother. I think it's Go Fish.

I'm a bit upset because I am about to lose. I stand up and tell her I don't want to play anymore.

Ian whispered, "We are witnessing the dawn of the Dawn we know today."

"That is true," she confirmed with a nod. "I never liked losing. Still don't."

"This is a great start. Now, clear your mind and tell us when something arises," Dream Weaver instructed.

"Oh, this was not me at my best. But for the record, I was being honest."

"Let's have it," said Carter.

I am in first grade. I go to the grocery store to pick something up with my dad. A girl from school is outside selling homemade brownies for a fundraiser. My dad bought me one, and I take a bite before leaving the table. I can't believe it. How does someone goof up brownies? They are disgusting; I tell her how bad they are.

My exact words are, "Gross, you call this a brownie? You should throw these away and try again."

"You told her they were disgusting?" asked Scarlett with a look of dismay.

"Dawn, calling it like it has been since she was a kid," Ian added.

"I was trying to be helpful. She needed to know. Although I felt bad when she started to cry, in my defense, I was trying to save other hapless customers from paying to eat one."

"Sounds legit," Ian said.

"I'm not sure that was her takeaway," Carter muttered.

"Moving on. Clear your mind and create the space for something to arise," Dream Weaver guided.

Dawn let out a small chuckle.

> I'm about ten years old, and I see myself at camp. I'm having a great day, but I don't think the counselors would agree.
>
> My cabin is heading to arts and crafts, and I'm not an arts and crafts kid. I want to go to the lake and take out a kayak. So, I do.
>
> I'm having a great time watching some turtles and I even find a few frogs.
>
> The camp administrators are *not* having a great time. Unbeknownst to me, they made announcements on the loudspeaker and mobilize the counselors to look for me. They go on a search with walkie-talkies. Evidently, when campers go missing, it's a big deal. Who knew?

"Ummmm, everyone?" Carter replied.

"Hey, they weren't doing what I wanted, so I took it upon myself to fix it. My parents were paying good money for me to be there. Who were they to tell me what to do?"

"Uhhhhh, the counselors who were entrusted with your safety," Carter answered.

"I see that now!"

"The Force is strong with this one," announced Ian in his best Darth Vader voice.

"Your spirit shines brightly," confirmed Dream Weaver. "Let us continue on this path with conviction and purpose."

Dawn sat quietly, then began.

I've got something. I'm in seventh-grade history class. We've been assigned a group project to create a presentation about a historical figure. We have to share different aspects of this person's life, such as their achievements and impact. The final presentation will be in front of the class and can include posters or a short skit.

My team selects Leonardo Da Vinci. I am supposed to report on his many inventions. Someone else will talk about his artwork, and the third person in our group will cover science and anatomy.

Everything starts out okay. We divide roles and responsibilities and get to work—or at least, I get to work. At our first meeting, I discover no one else has done anything. I tell them to get started and explain what I expect them to have completed by the next meeting. But when the next meeting comes, they still haven't gotten very far.

The presentation is coming up soon, and I'm frustrated. I take over and do the whole thing. The only problem is that I don't think to make a clean handoff to my classmates. As they are presenting, it becomes apparent they didn't study the content I gave them. So, about halfway through, I take over and present their parts. My fellow team members get mad at me, and the teacher isn't happy with any of us. After everything I did, we don't even get a good grade. I am annoyed with everyone.

"I don't know how you do it," Scarlett said. "You just take charge when there's a void of leadership."

"And sometimes, when there isn't a void," Ian joked.

"Yeah. It drives me crazy when people don't step up."

"Sounds like something we might consider during your vision quest when we look to the future," Dream Weaver said. "For now, let's move a little forward in time."

Dawn quieted her mind and allowed a new story to emerge.

"Okay. I'm not too proud of this one. But hey, I got what I wanted."

"Set aside your judgments and speak from the heart," Dream Weaver instructed.

It's my freshman year in high school and I'm trying out for the school play. I want to be the lead, a kick-ass character. Instead, I'm given a minor role and cast as the lead's understudy. It becomes obvious to me, and I would assume everyone else, that I am far better than her. This pisses me off. I feel like they chose her because she is a senior, not because she's better. I'm sure she knew it, too.

So, I take it upon myself to help her out. I give her lots of useful suggestions. Then, right before the dress rehearsal, I give her some feedback to fix her biggest issues, which, for some reason, freaks her out. She forgets a lot of her lines and walks off stage. On opening night, she has a panic attack, and I get to play the lead after all.

"Did you regret giving her advice?" Scarlett asked.

"Not at the time, though I feel a little bad about it now."

"That's growth!" Ian proclaimed.

"I suppose. But I did get to play the lead."

Carter placed his hand on his forehead in disbelief. "Let's put a pin in this topic for the vision quest."

Dream Weaver nodded. "We have time for one last adventure before we pause for a brief rest."

The influence of the Memory Stones seemed to be weakening, and Dawn took a while before speaking.

Ahhhh. Here we go. It is my junior year of high school, and I'm a member of the student council. We're discussing the shirts we're going to order for our pep rally. Our school colors are yellow and blue and there are three factions: Those who want to order yellow shirts with blue writing, those who are lobbying for blue shirts with yellow writing, and those who want gray shirts with blue and yellow writing.

I don't care. A shirt is a shirt. I hang in there for a while. But after fifteen minutes, I can't take it anymore. We have bigger fish to fry, and we need to decide. The committee leader allows the conversation to go on way too long, so, I end it. 'That's it. We are going with white shirts with blue and yellow writing.'

I think I said it so forcefully that nobody wanted to disagree, and we just went with it. I have no patience for the little stuff.

"The more things change…" Ian winked.

"I have to agree with you on that one," Dawn acknowledged.

"You have done well. Now, let us rest, and when we return, we will walk the path into your adult years," Dream Weaver said.

Reflections on the Level 1 Eagle

When Dawn begins her journey, we see the first signs of an Eagle at the Unevolved State. Dawn knew what she wanted her dog's name to be, and her mind was not changing. Eagles are bold and fiercely independent. But that can manifest as stubbornness at this stage. Driven by an unwavering sense of self-reliance and a strong will, they approach challenges with single-minded determination that can border on inflexibility.

PIQ1 Eagles will go to great lengths to avoid losing. Their drive to win can show up in games, sports, or even casual discussions that they turn into debates. They may disregard the rules to achieve victory.

Just as Dawn walked away from the game with her grandmother, PIQ1 Eagles may do anything, including "bending the rules," to avoid losing. They might even accuse others of cheating or change the rules of the game on the fly. And if they do lose, they may not accept the loss. You might hear them say something like, "Not in my book," or they may make up a story to claim victory based on unusual circumstances or technicalities.

The overriding wish to be perceived as authoritative inhibits their willingness to be vulnerable. They may struggle to express their feelings, which can inhibit emotional intimacy and the formation of meaningful connections. Ultimately, this can lead to loneliness and isolation.

Next, we see Dawn's communication style in action when she gives feedback to her brownie-making schoolmate. PIQ1 Eagles typically value truth over diplomacy and sensitivity. They communicate frankly, but sometimes to the point of being harsh or abrasive. They may not soften their words or cushion potentially hurtful statements, prioritizing honesty over maintaining harmony in relationships. While they intend to be honest or efficient, they may be perceived as insensitive or even rude, especially to those with the Dove style.

In high-pressure situations, communicating respectfully can be a challenge for unevolved Eagles. They may speak with certainty and tell people what to do, even if it is not their place. They might use phrases such as "You should," "We must," or "Here's what you need to do," and if they have positional power, they may stifle a free flow of ideas. Their spouse or staff may feel like a decision has already been made, so what's the point in arguing or expressing one's view? Their communication style may be described as commanding.

At this stage, Eagles tend to believe that rules don't apply to them, as demonstrated when Dawn decided to go kayaking on her own. They often exhibit a rebellious streak and test boundaries, unconstrained by convention or how people might react. When their disregard for rules is paired with impulsiveness, it can lead to reckless actions.

This can lead to dangerous situations for young Eagles, while adult PIQ1 Eagles might make decisions without considering the long-term implications. Combine an Eagle's extreme confidence with the belief that rules are just suggested guidelines, and the result is someone who may overestimate their abilities.

Dawn's taking over the school project and doing everything herself illustrates various aspects of her style. Eagles at this level are repelled by inaction, which drives them to take charge of things. They fear that otherwise, they won't achieve their goals. In turn, they take responsibility for things that are not theirs to own. Upon seeing a problem, unevolved Eagles may assume that only they can fix it. This is especially true if something takes longer than they think it should, or if a solution seems obvious. So, they jump in and own the problem, and judge others for being unable to solve the problem themselves.

After taking charge, PIQ1 Eagles may view themselves as heroic leaders who have come to save the day. Unfortunately, this becomes disempowering, as others lose the chance to gain the confidence and skills to take ownership. Thus, the Eagle must take over if the circumstances arise again.

Unevolved Eagles project an unwavering belief in themselves. When they feel doubt, they may double down on their conviction. Essentially, they overcompensate for their lack of ability by expressing deep conviction to cover for their lack of competence. They typically don't take responsibility for their actions when things go wrong. Instead, they shift the blame to external circumstances.

When Dawn got to play the lead in the school play, she didn't consider the feelings of the student cast to play the lead. While she didn't intentionally sabotage the lead actor, her ambition overrode all emotional concerns. She was focused only on her time to shine.

Similarly, when Dawn decided on the color of the high school T-shirts, she demonstrated a lack of patience. The unevolved Eagle has little patience for triviality. They care about the big things and can't be bothered by the small stuff.

But this is just the beginning of Dawn's journey. Let's see how she evolves.

The Level 2 Eagle

After the Fire Keeper re-energized the Memory Stones, everyone gathered in the Nest. "Let us all return to focusing on our breath as Dawn prepares to bring forth her next adventure," said Dream Weaver.

It didn't take long for the stones to work their magic. Dawn winced, and the group waited in anticipation. "This was not one of my shining moments. But in retrospect, it's pretty funny."

> I've just gotten married, and my first house is a bit of a fixer-upper. I need to install a faucet and even though I've never installed one before, I am sure I can figure it out. As for instructions, who needs them? It seems pretty obvious. I buy a new faucet and collect some tools. I am eager to begin, so I unscrew the old faucet.
>
> That's when I discover how much water pressure we have in the house. For the record, it's a lot. I don't know what to do first. I try to hold the geyser back with the palm of my hand, but it's too strong. Then, I frantically fumble to turn off the water. The kitchen is drenched.
>
> I'm still hearing about it.

"That's pretty awesome," said Ian.

"I think we define *awesome* differently," Carter said. "At no point did you consider reading the instructions first?"

"What are these instructions of which you speak?" Dawn asked with a grin.

Carter just shook his head as everyone had a good laugh. Then, without missing a beat, Dawn continued, "Here's another one I'm not too proud of, but it's coming through, so I'll share it."

"You're in a no-judgment zone," Dream Weaver said.

> I just started working at my first real job after college. The company has a perk that employees don't have to work on their birthday. Sounds great, right?
>
> But many people are unhappy with it, feeling it's unfair to those whose birthdays fall on a Saturday or Sunday. It's just not right that they don't get to capitalize on the perk. I figure I can become a folk hero by securing an extra day off for those with weekend birthdays. Unfortunately, it doesn't quite turn out as planned.
>
> The owner feels like he created that perk to be nice, and if it makes people unhappy, he'll get rid of it. So, he does. No more days on your birthday. I was trying to help, but I end up becoming the villain. Nobody likes the villain.
>
> I didn't stay there long after that.

"Your intentions were honorable. We can revisit this later. For now, let's move forward. My intuition tells me to ask you about a recent vacation," Dream Weaver said.

Dawn thought about it momentarily, then began describing her trip to California with her family.

> I have a goal to see all the main attractions, so I create an ambitious agenda. Our flight arrives early, and we go right to Hollywood to see the Walk of Fame. We snap a few photos of the stars of our favorite actors. It's a good start—Walk of Fame accomplished.

> Then we do a quick drive-by of the Hollywood sign, and from there, we go to the Griffith Observatory. We don't have time to go in because our itinerary is jam-packed, but at least we get to see it and the fantastic view. We then cruise down Sunset Boulevard and check out the Venice Beach Boardwalk. That place is wild. We take in a quick view of the ocean, watched the skateboarders for a few minutes, then go to Rodeo Drive for some window shopping. The day ends with a short visit to the Getty Center to soak in the art and panoramic views. I doubt anyone could cover more ground. And that is just day one!

Carter's jaw had dropped. "I could have spent an entire day at either the Griffin Observatory or the Getty Center. I feel like you missed a lot."

"Missed a lot? We *saw* a lot!"

"Maybe we all have different perspectives of what a vacation should be," Scarlett said.

"I think we got a sense of what happened there. Now, clear your mind and allow what wants to arise to come forth," Dream Weaver said.

Ahhhh. Here's a small one, but it is quite poignant. After our busy season at work, I could tell a lot of people were stressed out. Since we exceeded our goals, I think it could be a great idea to hold a team building day. We hire a company and work together to solve various problems. In one of the activities, we are discussing solutions to save the world from an alien invasion, and I share mine. The team immediately agrees to go with my plan. To my surprise, one of my folks turns to me and asks, "How do you know that's how to do this?"

I reply, "I don't. I was just sharing an idea."

At that point, another teammate erupts, "Wait a minute! You don't *know* that's the solution? You just *think* it's a good idea?"

My team member explains that she agreed to my solution because I said it so confidently, it seemed like I *knew* that it was the right solution. I had shared the idea with such conviction that it seemed like I had done this before, which convinced everyone to go with my solution.

The group returned to the drawing board and selected a different idea.

"What did you learn from that experience?" Dream Weaver asked.

"I realized that I must be careful how I share ideas with my team. My confidence combined with my role as the manager makes my ideas sound like decisions rather than suggestions."

"That's a great insight," Dream Weaver replied. "Let's see where else your spirit takes you."

Dawn felt nothing else was forthcoming. But then her eyes went wide.

This happened a few months ago.

Our company headquarters is in an office complex with eight buildings. As we grew, we leased another building, then another, and another. At this point, we occupy five of them.

One day, a team member noticed in our town paper that the landlord has rezoned the property for housing. Our lease is up in six months, which is a bad sign.

We panic. What if we get kicked out? We would not only lose our individual offices but also our production facility. This is a potential disaster.

I can't say that I enjoy a crisis, but the whole thing energizes me. While everyone else is spinning their wheels, I kick into gear. Within six weeks, I find a new building just two miles away and form a team to coordinate the move. And thank goodness I did. When it comes time to renew our lease, the landlord informed us that the property has been sold, and the buildings will be torn down later that year and replaced with condos.

"That's impressive," Carter said. "I don't know how you made that happen so fast."

"You just do it," Dawn replied.

"It's more like *you* just do it. I couldn't have done that. I would have needed to conduct months of research before making any decisions," Carter said.

"Dawn has indeed progressed on her path," Dream Weaver said. "This is a good place to rest our thoughts. Let us step outside and let the Fire Keeper tend to his duties. When we return, we will turn our eyes to the journey Dawn has yet to travel."

Reflections on the Level 2 Eagle

The Eagle's belief in themselves and their ideas can blind them to their own limitations, as Dawn learned when she attempted to install a new faucet. Their confidence may lead them to overlook important details or dismiss new information that challenges their perspective. This rigidity can also affect their personal development and damage their relationships.

Eagles are willing to fight for what they believe in, however, at Level 2, they don't always know which battles to pick. When Dawn fought for the extra day off for birthdays that fall on weekends, she didn't think through the implications of her actions. She stood up for her beliefs, which is a natural aptitude of the Eagle, but it cost all her coworkers that time off.

PIQ2 Eagles sometimes have difficulty relaxing, which Dawn's vacation illustrated. They turn leisure into a competition where whoever sees the most attractions wins. They might post on social media, "Another vacation in the books," as if they unlocked a new level in a vacation video game.

Eagles may find it difficult to unplug from work when on vacation. If you've ever stood in line at an amusement park and seen a parent check their email or take a business call—rather than engage with their family—that individual is possibly an Eagle at PIQ1 or PIQ2. They seek to use their time efficiently since they "aren't doing anything else" during that time, but that is family time they aren't present for. Simply having a conversation can be meaningful for both the Eagle and their child.

At this stage, Eagles speak with certainty and command respect. Their confidence can come across as dismissive of other perspectives, stifling alternative viewpoints and input. We saw this when Dawn shared her idea in the team building activity, and her coworkers perceived it as the "right" answer, not just a suggestion. A domineering Eagle can create an environment where people are hesitant to contribute and begin to feel undervalued and unheard. The lack of dialogue and diverse thinking drains a team of innovation, adaptability, and willingness to debate big decisions.

Tackling unexpected challenges is one of the Eagle's greatest abilities. From the Eagle's perspective, why waste a perfectly good crisis? When her company faced losing its lease, Dawn stayed focused and jumped into action. PIQ2 Eagles can make quick decisions and are able to shut out fear or other emotions that may inhibit action. They don't look forward to a crisis, but can thrive when it occurs. Eagles at this level may activate their leadership skills and take charge, regardless of whether they have the authority to do so.

At Level 2, Eagles operate at a fast pace. This can lead to impressive accomplishments, but it can also cause them to rush, overlook input, and make avoidable errors.

The Level 3 Eagle

After the group stretched their legs and returned to the warmth of the Nest, Dream Weaver spoke. "Now is the time for Dawn to walk toward a future where balance is hers to create. As with Ian, Dawn needs your help to face the forces that pull within her spirit. When you are ready, speak of what sets Dawn apart and how her path may bring deeper meaning to herself and the world."

"Candor," said Ian without hesitation. "I appreciate how Dawn speaks her mind and calls it like it is."

"Wonderful," Dream Weaver said. "What would help Dawn balance this gift?"

"Respect," answered Scarlett. "It's essential to be honest, but that should be balanced with empathy and consideration for the feelings of others."

"Beautiful," Dream Weaver said. "Other strengths?"

"Confidence," Ian replied. "I've always joked that nobody believes in Dawn more than Dawn."

"That confidence fuels her success," Carter added. "But I would suggest that it be balanced with humility."

"And vulnerability," Scarlett said. "When confident people allow themselves to be vulnerable, it makes them more approachable."

"Keep it going," Dream Weaver urged.

"Dawn has incredible drive. It's helped her advance quickly in her career and has pushed her to succeed since the day I met her," Ian said.

Dawn exhaled loudly, venting her exhaustion. "Yeah, but sometimes it would be nice to relax and just let go. I have to take the time to enjoy the little things. Like vacations."

"Yes!" Dream Weaver exclaimed. "Now, you're getting it. What else?"

"I've always respected Dawn's independence. She doesn't seem to need people like I do," Scarlett said.

"But I wouldn't get so burnt out at work if I trusted people more. I think I'm a team player, but I could bring that into greater balance."

"Wonderful," Dream Weaver said.

"I've always been impressed by how quickly Dawn reacts to problems," Carter added.

"Sometimes, it gets me in trouble. I've been thinking that I need to respond instead of react."

"Describe the difference," Dream Weaver requested.

"If I slow down and think before I speak or act, I'll probably make better decisions and offend people a little less."

"Or a lot less," Ian jabbed.

"Or a lot less," Dawn confirmed with a nod.

"I think this relates to the speed at which Dawn operates," Ian added. "And truth be told, this is one of my challenges as well. Dawn makes fast decisions and works quickly. But that can lead to mistakes."

The group was deep in thought when Scarlett asked, "I have another one. Is it okay to share it?"

"Of course," Dream Weaver replied.

"I am in awe of Dawn's ability to take charge and get things done. She seems to emerge as a leader in every group. But I wonder if, sometimes, that prevents other leaders from emerging."

"It probably does," Dawn admitted.

"This is wonderful," Dream Weaver said. "What you have shared offers Dawn a path to finding balance in her life. You have given her much to ponder on her way to being the highest expression of her spirit. Let's take a few minutes to recharge. When we return, we will begin with you, Carter."

Reflections on the Level 3 Eagle

Individuals with the Eagle style seek to accomplish goals quickly. They must slow down their thoughts, words, and actions if they are to attain a higher level of Personality Intelligence. Doing so can deepen their emotional awareness and prevent them from being triggered into conflict and aggression.

PIQ2 Eagles may experience intense emotions such as disappointment, impatience, frustration, and anger, especially in stressful situations. To progress to PIQ3, Eagles must tame their intensity, relax, and maintain composure. By balancing their compulsion to act with some Dove calm, they can make better decisions and communicate more respectfully.

Eagles at PIQ2 tend to focus intensely on the bottom line and lack patience. By slowing down and being more present for others, Eagles can show that they care and truly listen, leading to deeper connection. Pumping the brakes also prevents them from rushing through conversations, skipping details, and charging headlong into action.

A steadier, unhurried state of mind can also take the sharp edge off of Eagle communication. This shift enables them to present ideas as options rather than decisions. By being more mindful of their tone and the potential impact of their words, Eagles reduce the risk of offending others and balance their intensity with respect and congeniality.

Slowing down also enables Eagles to connect with positive emotions like serenity, joy, and gratitude, resulting in a more positive mindset and healthier relationships. By chilling out, Eagles become more receptive to other people's ideas and more attuned to the potential impact of their words and decisions.

By balancing the great strengths of the Eagle style with their opposite, Eagles truly step into their power.

Real-Life Level 3 Eagles

Arnold Schwarzenegger

Everything about Arnold Schwarzenegger screams Eagle. Assertive, direct, and driven to achievement. The "Austrian Oak" first gained notoriety by winning the title of Mr. Universe at age twenty, just five years after he began lifting weights, and Mr. Olympia seven times.

That insatiable will to grow—literally—and win came through in Arnold's 1977 autobiography (a very Eagle thing to publish at age thirty): "For me life is continuously being hungry. The meaning of life is not simply to exist, to survive, but to move ahead, to go up, to achieve, to conquer."

And conquer he did. When Schwarzenegger took up acting in the 1980s, agents and casting people didn't take him seriously because of his accent and long name. "Basically, everywhere I turned I was told that I had no chance," Schwarzenegger recounts. "But this only made me more determined and inspired me to work harder. I took acting and voice classes, and I never gave up."

That is exactly how an Eagle responds to naysayers. Oh, I can't do that? Watch me. As he said, "So, the trick is to learn how to utilize and optimize who you are as an individual and not worry about what or who everyone else wants you to be." Being independent of the feelings of others is part of the Eagle recipe for success (when used within reason).

The casting agents eventually put Schwarzenegger in the most Eagle lead roles imaginable, in *Conan the Barbarian* and

The Terminator. His character's catchphrases—"I'll be back," "Get to the chopper!" and "Come with me if you want to live"— are pure Eagle.

Schwarzenegger's achievements as Governor of California and founder of multiple nonprofits speak to his Eagle will to achieve, yet he embraced Dove traits that differentiate a Level 3 Eagle. His Dove humility comes through in a 2017 commencement speech at the University of Houston: "None of us can make it alone. None of us," said Schwarzenegger, adding later, "I always tell people that you can call me anything that you want ... But don't ever, ever call me the self-made man."

Level 1 Eagles believe they are the cause of all their successes (and none of their failures), and even Level 2 Eagles may recognize the contributions of others but still see themselves as the real hero. At Level 3, though, Eagles don't need the myths they once told about themselves or that others told. In the commencement speech, Schwarzenegger credits family members, teachers, coaches, mentors, colleagues, role models, friends, and the United States itself for enabling his successes. His decision to support programs like the Special Olympics and after-school programs for disadvantaged youth stemmed from a Dove duty to pay it forward.

Arnold gave the speech like an Eagle—as a firm, confident recounting of accomplishments. But the lesson was Dove: "...as soon as you understand that you are here because of a lot of help, then you also understand that now is [the] time to help others. That's what this is all about." He directed the students to thank everyone who helped them become college graduates—and give back.

Simone Biles

At the 2020 Tokyo Olympics (held in 2021), American gymnast Simone Biles was favored to medal in all her events. She would compete but eventually withdrew. An Eagle with immense risk tolerance, Biles had pushed the limits of her sport with routines that no other gymnasts even dared to try in competition. But in Tokyo, she struggled to execute.

Suffering from the "twisties," a lack of spatial awareness in the air, Biles realized she was jeopardizing her team's medal count and risking a career-ending injury. Despite being team captain, she pulled out of the remaining events (except the beam finals). Her critics were relentless, accusing her of lacking mental toughness and commitment. *America hates me. The world is going to hate me*, she recalled thinking. Nevertheless, she supported her teammates for the rest of the games, refusing to hide in shame the way a Level 1 or 2 Eagle might have.

That's Level 3 Eagle—they can set aside ego and channel Dove humility and empathy when the moment requires. They can balance their drive to win by tapping into the Dove's self-reflectiveness. In moments where a reckless, charge-ahead style would only find trouble, a Level 3 Eagle can step back, think, and then act with resolve, as Biles did in Tokyo.

Following the 2020 Games, Biles took a two-year break from competing. Commentators wondered whether she'd ever return to the sport, let alone enter another Olympics. She did both, demonstrating the mental resilience critics had accused her of lacking. She was also open about what it took to rebuild trust in herself. Biles began to see a therapist. In the gym, she relearned her movements on soft surfaces and ball pits. It takes an advanced Eagle to exercise that caution and restraint, especially when doing something that was once second nature.

Like Schwarzenegger, Biles also expresses deep gratitude to the people who made her success possible. Biles grew up in the foster care system while her mother struggled with substance abuse, and her grandparents, Nellie and Ron, adopted her at age six. "Thanks for making sacrifices since Day 1 so I can live out my dream," Biles shared in a 2021 Instagram post thanking them. It was one of many such moments she has taken to publicly acknowledge their support.

Biles demonstrates Level 3 Eagle traits outside of competition too. In testimony to Congress, she bravely shared her story of being sexually abused by USA Gymnastics doctor Larry Nasser. "I don't want another young gymnast, or Olympic athlete, or any individual to experience the horror that I and hundreds of others have endured before, during, and continuing to this day in the wake of the Larry Nassar abuse," told Congress. Her Eagle resolve to stand up to evil came from a place of compassion and concern for fellow gymnasts.

In 2024, after winning her second gold in Paris, Biles put on a diamond-studded necklace of a goat. It was a play on GOAT, or greatest of all time. "The haters hate it, so I love that even more," Biles told the press. With a record-setting eleven Olympic medals and thirty World Championship medals, Biles is, undisputedly, the GOAT of women's gymnastics. And if Biles is any indication, all Eagles—regardless of their level—love having opponents and detractors. It brings out their best.

Chapter 12:
The Owl

The Level 1 Owl

The Fire Keeper reset the Memory Stones with care, and the group returned to their places on the Nest floor. Ian turned to Carter. "You're up! Are you ready?"

"I suppose so," Carter replied with a hint of trepidation.

Carter retrieved a first-aid kit from his bag.

Ian spoke for the remaining friends, who all looked confused. "Why a first-aid kit?"

The question created a bit of cognitive dissonance for Carter, as he felt that it was obvious. "Well, it's practical and represents that I am prepared for anything."

"Is that the same first-aid kit that saved me from certain death?" Ian asked.

"It is the same kit that I have taken with me since I was a young child. So, yes. It is the kit that I brought with us on our camping trip."

"Let us begin," Dream Weaver spoke softly, her voice carrying the wisdom of the old ways. "Close your eyes, my children, and breathe deeply. Tune into the energy of your focus object and let your breath flow like the wind through the pines. Be still, be calm, like the quiet waters of the mountain lake, where the spirit finds peace."

It took time for Carter to quiet his thoughts and reach a place where the stories began to surface. "I'm not sure if I am doing this right, but I think I have a story to share."

"There is no right or wrong," Dream Weaver said. "There is only what is. Please," she gestured with an open palm. And Carter, measured and precise, began.

> I would estimate I am six years old, lying in bed. I've lost a tooth and have some questions about the Tooth Fairy.
>
> Nothing about it makes sense to me. I mean, how does she know when I've lost my tooth? And how does she get into my house? Is there just one Tooth Fairy or many of them? And if there is one, how does she get to all the houses in one night? Santa has reindeer. What does she have? Wings? Does she fly? And what does she do with the teeth? So. Many. Questions.
>
> The next morning, I wake up and find a five-dollar bill under my pillow. But the interesting thing is that it is accompanied by a letter. And *that* is a clue.

The handwriting seems strangely familiar. I just have to test my hypothesis. I find something my mother wrote and compare it to the Tooth Fairy's handwriting, and voila, it's a perfect match!

"Wait a minute," Dawn said. "You reverse-engineered the Tooth Fairy?"

"Well, technically, you would reverse-engineer something to understand how it works and then replicate it. I had no intention of becoming a Tooth Fairy. This was investigative work."

"This is gold," Ian declared. "Pure gold."

Dream Weaver seemed amused and had to gather herself before asking everyone to do the same. She fanned herself with the branch a few times then asked Carter to continue.

He took a few deep breaths then spoke. "Something is coming in. I want to allow it to come in fully before I share it."

The group waited until Carter nodded and began.

Okay. I'm in fourth grade. The school is painting a giant mural spanning an entire hallway, and each grade contributes a section.

Each grade has specific times they are supposed to paint. I spend days working out what I am going to add. My grade's time arrives.

The problem is that we have to finish our classwork before painting and, as usual, it takes me a long time to finish. So, when I get there, there isn't much left to do. All I get to do is color in the trunk of a tree. I am extremely disappointed.

When I get home, my parents are furious at the teacher, and my mother writes her a note, but I can't help but feel that it was my fault.

"You often take a little longer to do things than most, but that's how you produce such high-quality work," Scarlett reassured her friend.

"I see a theme we may wish to revisit in the vision quest," said Dream Weaver, who then advised Carter, "It seems like you are re-experiencing the events rather than just watching them. Separate yourself from the story and be the observer."

"I understand," he replied. Carter composed himself and gathered his thoughts. Now that he had the hang of it, the next scene appeared quickly.

Here's something I've always regretted. You all know that I play piano.

I'm in fifth grade, and we're having a talent show. My parents suggest that I enter the contest, but I'm reluctant. I want to do it, but there is a girl with an amazing voice participating, and I don't think I can compete with that. There is also a group of kids who are class comedians doing a skit that is a riff on the Pepto Bismol commercial. I see a preview, and it is hilarious. I can't compete with that either. So, I don't do it.

After all, why do something if you know other people will be better? I always wished I had done it, though.

Looking back, they probably weren't any better than I was. But there was a little voice that, at the time, wasn't so little, that kept telling me I wouldn't measure up. I always wondered what might have been, not at the talent show but for me as a piano player. I think there is an alternate timeline in the multiverse where there is a version of me living the life of a rock star, touring the world and playing music. But that was not meant to be.

"We all have regrets," Scarlett said. "It's only human."

"Thank you for sharing your story," Dream Weaver spoke with gentle wisdom. "Regrets are like threads that bind us to the past and restrain us from walking freely in the present. Today, you can let those threads fall away."

Although uncertainty lingered, Carter nodded, wanting to believe Dream Weaver's words.

"You are on the path," Dream Weaver affirmed. "Let more stories come forth, like leaves carried by the breeze."

Before long, Carter shared his next memory.

Ahhhh, here's one I'd rather forget.

I'm in seventh grade and my teacher is a bit unorganized. Fortunately, he provides a class calendar, so we know what is coming up. For weeks,

I am excited that we are going to do a project based on the scientific method. I am fascinated by it. I know my career will be in the sciences, so this is important for my development.

Inexplicably, my teacher forgets to assign the scientific method project to us.

Someone had to tell him.

"Oh, no. You didn't?" Ian said with a facepalm.

"Of course, I did. Someone had to tell him. And as you can well imagine, that made me instantly popular with the entire class."

"I can see why your fellow students didn't like that," Scarlett said.

"The irony is, I thought my classmates would appreciate me pointing it out. I figured they were upset about it, too. Well, let's just say I ate a lot of lunches alone until they got over it."

"Perhaps something else we will revisit in the vision quest. But for now, let us journey forward," Dream Weaver gently offered. "Walk to the days of your teens or early twenties. Let us see what comes to greet you."

Carter's eyes grew wide. "Ian, you're going to like this one; you're in it."

"Ooooh, my favorite stories!"

In college, I usually went to the library when I had to work on a project. I liked the quiet.

On this day, it's storming outside, and I don't want to get wet, so I am writing a five-page paper in the dorm room I share with Ian. We're in the same philosophy class, so we have the same assignment.

We both sit down to work, and Ian starts typing. I am collecting my thoughts and trying to outline them on paper, but Ian is writing his paper—literally writing it. No structure. No plan. He just starts. After about half an hour, he has written a page and a half of content. Meanwhile, I have a series of ideas that I need to organize. I am working it out in my head, but he is already a quarter of the way there.

I couldn't believe it.

"How else would you do it?" Ian asked. "You just start typing and the words appear. You can always clean them up later."

"That's not how I work. Before I commit to that first word, I need the entire plan."

"Yeah, but you didn't start writing for like two hours!"

"True. But what I wrote required little editing."

Ian laughed. "We are so different."

Dream Weaver spoke. "You certainly are and how wonderful that is. I sense the spirit of this place calls for us to rest. We shall reconvene when Fire Keeper tells us it is time."

Reflections on the Level 1 Owl

Owls have questions. Lots of them. The Tooth Fairy story shows us that even at a young age, PIQ1 Owls need to understand the world around them. They have a low tolerance for ambiguity and want data. Lots of data. Carter's parents probably wanted to carry on with the myth of the Tooth Fairy, but Carter wasn't having it. First-level Owls tend to ask, "Why?" a lot. So much so that it can frustrate others and lead unevolved Owls down rabbit holes. Ever been in a work meeting that keeps circling back to the same question, over and over, from slightly different angles, and no answer is good enough? That's likely a Level 1 Owl at work.

When Carter didn't get the chance to contribute fully to the school mural, he displayed one of the critical challenges of PIQ1 Owls: the prioritization of quality over speed. At this stage, Owls establish impossibly high standards. This perfectionistic mindset can lead to frustration and feelings of inadequacy when things do not go according to plan. Good enough for the unevolved Owl is not good enough. It is a failure. And if they fail, they hold onto it, which might hurt their self-esteem.

Elevated expectations played out again when Carter did not enter the talent show. His loud internal critic, typical of the PIQ1 Owl, kept him from taking risks and using his talents. This negative self-talk can lead to self-doubt, which can undermine confidence, foster feelings of inadequacy, and fuel anxiety.

Over time, this inner voice can become a barrier to personal growth. Fear of failure and relentless self-judgment can make it so hard to appreciate one's successes that fulfillment and satisfaction remain out of reach.

For Owls at this stage, perfection quiets the inner voice. After all, if it's perfect; there's nothing to criticize. And perfection comes from adherence to structure and rules. PIQ1 Owls find comfort in having clear expectations to meet. When Carter's teacher deviated from the pre-established plan, the disruption threw a wrench in Carter's plan. How could he possibly become a scientist if he skipped this vital step? At this level, breaking from the plan is unnerving and creates anxiety.

Finally, we see Carter and Ian writing papers for school. While Ian, the Parrot, kicks right into action, Carter requires a complete plan before he can write. If the Level 1 Owl does not have all the information, they may become paralyzed by inaction, trapped in a cycle of overthinking every aspect of what they are doing.

The Level 2 Owl

The Fire Keeper tended to the stones while the group rested, renewing their warmth and sacred force. With that task complete, Dream Weaver welcomed them to reconvene in the Nest. "Let us continue on this journey of discovery. When you are ready, Carter."

He closed his eyes and allowed new memories to surface as the stones reached full force. "Remember the first time we all went camping together?" Carter asked his three friends.

"How could we forget?" Ian replied. "That's when you saved my life."

"Well, I don't think I saved your life; maybe your little finger."

This story begins with my friend over there raining mockery upon me—yes, *you*, Ian.

Before our trip, I want to make sure that everyone is prepared, so, I make a packing list and send it to the group. It includes the usual items: moisture-wicking clothing, a raincoat, extra socks in case the ones we're wearing get wet—you know, the basics.

I also bring an emergency whistle, a tent repair kit, water filtration tablets in case we can't start a fire, bear spray, a first-aid kit, a headlamp, and a compass, just in case the battery-powered solar panel I am using to charge my phone fails to work.

On our first night out, Mr. Why-Do-We-Need-All-This-Stuff? decides to use his pocketknife to carve a piece of wood. And wouldn't you know it, the knife slips and plunges into his pinky finger. It is fascinating how much blood can come from such a little finger.

"Let me share what happened next," Ian interrupted, ignoring the Dream Weaver's look conveying *This is highly unusual but okay*. "Carter knew exactly what to do. He was first aid certified, of course. He applied pressure to stop the bleeding and wrapped my finger with bandages. This little piggy owes you!"

Dream Weaver was delighted by this story. "It sounds like you seek to do things properly, and that saved the day. Perhaps we will revisit that in the vision quest. Thank you for sharing, Ian, but let's return to Carter sharing his stories," she said with a wink.

"Fiiiiiiiine," Ian smirked. Carter filled the silence.

Here's another one. This only involves me.

It's time to get a new mattress, and since I will inevitably sleep on it for many years, I want to make the right decision. I meticulously compare the options, read countless reviews, analyze materials, and visit multiple stores to test different models. I create a spreadsheet detailing firmness levels, warranties, and customer feedback.

I can't decide between memory foam or a hybrid material. I'm not sure which will offer the best long-term comfort. Finally, I pick the ideal mattress. I feel really good about my choice, but I discover that I took too long and the model I selected has been discontinued.

I had to start all over again.

"Why couldn't you just get the new model that replaced the one you chose?" Dawn asked.

"And get an untested mattress? Who would do that?" Carter replied in disbelief.

Ian raised his hand halfway, signaling exactly who would do that, until Scarlett glared at him and he put his hand down.

Dawn asked, "How long did it take until you got a new mattress after that point?"

"It took a few weeks, but I am very happy with my decision."

"These moments are sacred on your life's journey. The look back informs the look ahead," Dream Weaver said. "Let us watch where your steps lead next. Take a deep breath and let the wisdom within you come forward."

Here we go. This one started poorly, but it had a happy ending.

I'm in college and meet someone in one of my classes; she asks me to join her at a party. I'm not a party guy, but she seems nice, and I figure it will give me a chance to get to know her. What I don't account for is that she is like a level-10 social butterfly. From the second we get there, she flits from person to person and group to group. I can't keep up.

I let her do her thing and leave her to mingle, but I don't know how to start a conversation and am concerned that once I get in one, I won't know how to end it. So, I just sit down on the couch. I am alone for a while, which is fine, but after a few minutes someone else joins me. We sit in silence for about ten minutes, which is also fine.

After I recharge for a bit, I ask my couch mate who she knows at the party. She points to her date, who is gesticulating wildly while talking to another woman, who, wouldn't you know it, is my date! We have a good laugh and spend the rest of the evening getting to know each other.

"What about the woman you went to the party with?" Scarlett asked.

"Oh, she ended up leaving with my new friend's date. It was for the best."

"Did you remain friends with the person you met at the party?" Ian asked.

"We hung out for a while but lost touch after graduating. But at least I made a friend that night."

"I like that story," said Scarlett. "Not everyone likes parties where they don't know anyone, but you made the best of it."

"I did. But it took a while," Carter said.

Feeling like the effect of the Memory Stones was weakening, Carter took a minute before he felt ready to share his next memory.

Here's something that happened last year at work.

I have a new employee on my team. It is her first job after graduating from college, so I take her under my wing.

For several months, I keep a log of everything she can improve on. I wish someone had done that for me, and I want to help her. When it comes time for her performance review, I sense she is nervous. I tell her not to worry and walk her through everything she can work on to do better next year.

That's when I notice she looks upset, and it hits me. I've only pointed out things she can work on and failed to mention what she is doing well. By the time the meeting is over, she leaves feeling good about her accomplishments and has a plan for doing even better the next year.

"This is a difficult one for me as well. It's hard to remember to compliment people for doing their job well. But you course-corrected when you saw she needed some positive feedback. Nicely done," Dawn said.

Dream Weaver offered, "There is a time to honor contributions and a time to nudge someone back to their path. That story shows me you have advanced on your journey. Let's move on. I believe there is time for one more story."

Carter sat quietly, uncertain if anything else would come. His cheeks tightened with pride and satisfaction.

My organization was eager to release an upgrade to our bestselling software.

We're on a tight deadline, and senior management is applying a lot of pressure. As the lead developer, I know we haven't conducted thorough testing before the launch. I've raised a variety of concerns, but I have encountered a lot of resistance from my boss, who is being pressured by the CEO to just ship it. He feels that if we have minor bugs, we can fix them with an update. I disagree.

I carefully lay out my case and convince enough people to delay the launch. And it's a good thing.

Right before the upgrade goes live, we discover a minor glitch in a single line of code that would have triggered a cascade of breakdowns and data losses. This could have been a multi-million-dollar disaster.

The extra weeks of testing not only safeguarded the company's reputation but potentially saved it.

"That is a beautiful story," Dream Weaver said. "Your mindful attention to detail served many. On that note, let's allow the Fire Keeper to do his work. When we resume, we will consider your future self."

Reflections on the Level 2 Owl

People with the Owl style are usually well-prepared for every possible outcome. Their attention to detail and thorough planning allows them to anticipate potential challenges and proactively develop strategies in case they happen. We saw this with Carter in his preparation for the camping trip.

In environments that require careful decision-making, such as work projects or emergencies, the PIQ2 Owl's meticulous nature can prevent costly mistakes and lead to well-informed outcomes. This quality also instills confidence in others, as Owls often become a source of guidance in complex or high-stakes situations.

The downside is that the Level 2 Owl's process can sometimes be time-consuming, causing delays or missed opportunities. The Owl's tendency to overanalyze things can lead to indecision, or "analysis paralysis," where the fear of making the wrong choice prevents any choice from being made at all. Balancing careful thought with timely action is vital to avoiding these pitfalls.

We saw this in action when Carter tried to select a new mattress. On the positive side, he thoroughly considered all options, reducing the likelihood of mistakes and increasing the likelihood of a good decision. On the less positive side, his analysis took so long that his first choice was no longer available. He'd spent many hours researching his purchase only to have to start again.

Another challenge faced by Owls at this stage is discomfort in unfamiliar surroundings or large groups. Because small talk lacks substance, in the Owl's view, it's not worth doing. When Carter went to the party, he preferred having one deep conversation to a series of short, surface-level interactions. On the bright side, Carter made a new friend. However, PIQ2 Owls will find that engaging in group conversation, deep or shallow, can benefit their personal and professional lives. Sometimes, small talk is the price of making meaningful connections.

When Carter provided feedback to his new team member, he initially focused only on areas of deficiency and neglected what she was doing well. PIQ2 Owls tend to focus on what is broken as opposed to what is working. This can make them appear nitpicky and demotivating if they focus on the twenty percent that was done poorly without acknowledging the eighty percent that was done well. This blind spot can make the Owl's coworkers, family members, and friends feel undervalued or overlooked.

This pattern also plays out when Level 2 Owls encounter new ideas. They may address the risks, flaws, and downsides without noting anything they like. This can create the perception that they dislike the idea when, in fact, they may support it despite some addressable shortcomings.

When Carter's team wanted to release software before it was fully tested, Carter showed how an Owl's thoroughness can save the day. PIQ2 Owls often ask questions that most people wouldn't think of and make sure everything is done correctly. If you are fortunate to have an Owl in your world, they will keep you safe and pay attention to the small things that could create significant problems.

The Level 3 Owl

After resting, the group gathered in the Nest. Dream Weaver spoke, "As we did for your companions, Ian and Dawn, we turn our attention to the path that Carter has yet to walk. Carter, this is the moment for you to embrace the spirit within you by understanding the harmony of all things—light and shadow, calm and storm. With the guidance of those around you, we will walk the path of the forces that seek balance within.

"Now, I ask you all to close your eyes and turn your gaze inward. See the capabilities that Carter shares with the world. When your heart is ready, speak them aloud, so your words bring them to life in our circle."

"I appreciate how Carter takes his time to make careful decisions," said Scarlett.

"True, but sometimes, he takes too long to move from thinking to acting. Carter could benefit from balancing analysis and planning with more decisiveness," Dawn added.

"I would cautiously agree with that," Carter winked.

"What else?" Dream Weaver asked.

Ian jumped in. "Carter's commitment to doing things right the first time—no, wait, not just right, but perfectly—blows me away. If you ask Carter to do something, it may take a while, but it will be awesome."

"What needs to be brought into balance?" Dream Weaver asked.

"Seek excellence, not perfection," Dawn said.

"That'll be challenging for me, but I'll try," Carter replied.

"How about this? I respect how Carter considers the facts before making decisions." Scarlett said.

"If I may," Ian offered. "He could balance that with decisions that come from the gut. I mean, your intuition is based on experience, and experience is a set of facts, right?

"I can get behind that," said Carter, pondering Ian's logic.

Silence filled the warm air while Scarlett seemed to rehearse and then edit an idea in her mind. "Sometimes I am willing to help you, but you seem to like doing things yourself," she said. "You could trust people more. You often take on the burden of doing things yourself."

"It's just that I know that if I do it, it will be done right," Carter explained.

"Would the world cease to turn if something is flawed?" Dream Weaver asked.

"It depends on the flaw," Carter joked. "But yeah, I see your point. My life would be easier if I trusted others to carry some of the load."

Scarlett had more to say. "I like how you have a process for everything. I've never met anyone with as many systems as you have. They must keep you organized."

"What if you let go of some of those systems and added in some flexibility and spontaneity?" Ian asked, leading the witness.

"Honestly, I've been working on that, but it's not as easy as you think," Carter replied.

"Winging it seems way easier than sticking to a plan," Ian grinned.

"Tell that to your pinky," said Dawn. "Let's not get rid of all his planning."

"There is wisdom in all that you have shared," said Dream Weaver. "This journey is about bringing our natural abilities into harmony, not merely swinging from one extreme to another. How about one more?"

Scarlett turned to Carter. "I've always felt you have a rich inner world. But sometimes, I wish you would share it with us. I can't always tell what you're feeling."

"You are not wrong," acknowledged Carter. "I usually keep my emotions to myself. I could be more open."

"On that note, I believe Carter's vision quest has reached its destination. Let us step out and allow the Fire Keeper to carry out his duties. When we return, we will shift our attention to Scarlett."

Reflections on the Level 3 Owl

Recall that in William Marston's model of personality, Owls perceive the world as hostile and believe they have less power than the world. To stay safe, they strive to control every aspect of their lives and work diligently to do everything perfectly. This approach shields them from criticism from those with more power.

At Level 3, Owls let go of the compulsion to control everything and fear of not doing so. This allows a healthier balance between speed and quality, intuition and data, independence and teamwork. While they continue to produce superior work, they can adapt swiftly to changes and complete projects on time or even ahead of schedule.

At PIQ3, Owls learn to trust the intuition and instinct rooted in years of experience. In so doing, they overcome the tendency to overanalyze, allowing them to be decisive. They also place trust in others, letting go of the need to handle everything on their own. They understand that things may not be perfect, and that's okay. In some situations, exactness matters, and in others, "good enough" is good enough. By setting more reasonable, practical standards, PIQ3 Owls are able to experience the satisfaction of success, which boosts their self-acceptance and self-esteem.

In addition, Level 3 Owls embrace the openness of trying things in new ways. They accept that letting go of established systems can lead to innovation and growth. While familiar structures provide comfort and stability, clinging to them too tightly may hinder adaptability and progress. By releasing rigid systems, Level 3 Owls become open to spontaneity, which can lead to unexpected discoveries. It also enables them to fully experience the world around them.

In relationships, Master Owls connect with their feelings and willingly express them. This vulnerability allows them to develop authentic relationships.

Though still attuned to risks, fears, and unintended consequences, the Master Owl can relax and let down their guard. That, in turn, can bring more richness and joy into their life.

Real-Life Level 3 Owls

Emma Watson

Hermione Granger is a quintessential Owl in the *Harry Potter* books and movies; this made the role a natural fit for actress Emma Watson. Her preparation to be Hermione—and really any character in any of her films—shows research, preparation, and attention to detail beyond the norm. Watson didn't just memorize *her* lines in Harry Potter; she memorized her co-stars' lines too. In outtakes from the first movie, she can be seen mouthing other actors' lines as they say them.

Similarly, before playing Belle in *Beauty and the Beast,* Watson went beyond learning lines. She underwent a whole "princess bootcamp" that involved lessons in horseback riding, formal dance, and singing. When Owls do anything, they do it thoroughly.

Level 3 Owls, however, don't just fit themselves to a task but discern how to extract greater depth and meaning from it. In Disney's 1991 animated *Beauty and the Beast*, Belle is the daughter of an inventor. In the 2017 version, Watson tweaked Belle's backstory to make her not just a voracious reader but an inventor herself. This Belle invents labor-saving devices so she can read *more*. That is an expression of Owl mastery. They don't just perfect things for perfection's sake; they channel that drive towards outcomes that allow more fun, joy, and excitement in their lives—traits we associate more with Parrots.

Like many Owls, Watson is hard on herself. During an appearance on *The Tonight Show Starring Jimmy Fallon*, Watson complimented Jimmy for his bit where parents tell children they ate their Halloween candy. Only, it was Jimmy Kimmel who does the bit. Fallon, a Parrot, brushed off the mistake and had Watson redo her entrance. Most Owls wouldn't like to relive that moment, yet years later, during another appearance on Fallon's show, Watson mentioned it herself, creating a comedic and memorable moment. Level 1 and 2 Owls are hard on themselves, but Level 3 Owls own their mistakes and find the humor in them, as Parrots often do.

As of this writing, Watson has not accepted a role in a movie for five years. Whereas a Parrot might take any chance to be on a screen, and an Eagle may feel pressure to keep their box office stats high, Watson has different priorities. "I think I felt a bit caged," she said, explaining her decision to step away. "The thing I found really hard was that I had to go out and sell something that I really didn't have very much control over." *Sooooo* Owl. She wanted to be more involved in "the process," she added.

And rather than view that issue as beyond her control, as a lower-level Owl might, Watson has taken command of her work life. She founded and now runs a gin company and has directed

Chapter 12: The Owl

Chapter 12: The Owl

commercials and music videos on her hiatus from acting. In addition, she has continued to advocate for women's rights and gender equality as a UN Women Goodwill Ambassador—a role she has held since 2014.

While Hermione Granger evolved in the *Harry Potter* movies, Watson has grown to exhibit the hallmarks of a Level 3 Owl. Though rumored to value her privacy and enjoy solitary pursuits, she does flip on the Parrot switch authentically. She is animated in TV interviews, using a full repertoire of facial expressions and hand movements to make her points. When meeting fans, she is authentically warm and friendly.

Like many stars on Instagram, Watson does the obligatory selfies and portraits. But overall, her image is usually not in her posts, which focus overwhelmingly on ideas, social issues, data points, and provocative quotes. A PIQ1 or PIQ2 Owl would do likewise, but Watson uses the loud visual design of a Parrot to get these concepts across. Text-dense Owl posts wouldn't have the same pop, or garner nearly seventy-four million followers, as Watson has.

Some Owls make no compromises with their desire for control and perfection. Though Watson has those same Owl needs, she's moderated them with Parrot lightness and fun, allowing change and growth in a career that is just getting started.

Neil deGrasse Tyson

Neil deGrasse Tyson is an Owl astrophysicist who could have lived a classic Owl life, head down at a computer studying telescope

– 223 –

imagery and running dizzyingly complex calculations. Instead, Tyson channeled his academic prowess into a career as a public intellectual that makes the complexity of the universe accessible and exciting for everyone. That takes Master Owl skill.

Tyson decided he wanted to become an astrophysicist at age nine after a visit to the Hayden Planetarium in New York. A lot of childhood dreams are just dreams, but high-level Owls like Tyson see and commit to their path from an early age. Thirty years after visiting Hayden, Neil deGrasse Tyson, PhD, with degrees from Harvard and Columbia, became its director.

Often, Level 2 Owls follow their career to a place of control and independence from arbitrary authority. That, perhaps, is why Owls are overrepresented in academia and likely to stay put after achieving tenure. In an interview with *Harvard Business Review*, Tyson explains his departure from that path: "Balance might be overrated. If your life is perfectly balanced—everything going smoothly—is it as dynamic as it could be? When life is out of balance, usually something is changing, and that's not always a bad thing. It gives you a new perspective. New projects always send things out of balance. I embrace disruptions to circumstances I've grown complacent about."

That might be the single best explanation from a Master Owl about how they embrace the Parrot style. Level 1 and 2 Owls want everything smooth and balanced. At Level 3, they show Tyson's appetite for novelty and disruption.

By Level 2, Owl experts learn to translate technical information into words laypeople can understand. A Level 3 Owl goes further, using Parrot-like storytelling to make technical concepts not only understandable but fascinating. For example, Tyson was once watching an NFL game in which a kicker barely made a field goal to win. Tyson posted on social media about how the Earth's rotation probably made the play a success. "I think people feel empowered when they learn a little more about how the world works," says Tyson, describing that instance. In essence, a PIQ3 Owl is more of a storyteller than a technical translator.

Tyson's attitude toward curiosity and science is telling as well. "History shows that if you let people go where their curiosity takes them, great things unfold," says Tyson. The term *great things* is quite Parrot.

In a moment that reflects both the Owl and Parrot styles, Neil deGrasse Tyson highlights a flaw in the movie *Titanic*: when Rose gazes up at the night sky, the stars are incorrect. He explains, "We know the exact day, time, longitude, latitude—everything about when and where that ship sank. There was only one sky she should have seen, and it was the wrong one. Worse, the left side of the sky was a mirror image of the right. It wasn't just wrong, it was lazy." The Owl in him spotted the inaccuracy, while the Parrot turned it into an entertaining story that had the audience laughing.

His incorporation of the Parrot style into his Owl shows up throughout his work. It's in the playful titles of his books, like *Death by Black Hole and Other Cosmic Quandaries* and *The Pluto Files: The Rise and Fall of America's Favorite Planet*. His social media posts also blend Owl and Parrot traits masterfully. For instance, Tyson managed to pinpoint the exact location of the *Barbie* movie's fictional world: "In @barbiethemovie, the Moon's orientation places Barbie World between 20 & 40 degrees North

Latitude on Earth. Palm trees further constrain latitude to between 20 & 30 degrees. The Sun & Moon rose and set over the ocean. If it's in the US, Barbie World lands somewhere in the Florida Keys."

And that is what makes a Level 3 Owl so beautiful. Even a random scene in a movie is filled with data points that lead to discovery and fun when Tyson applies his style to it.

Chapter 13:
The Dove

The Level 1 Dove

The Fire Keeper completed his work, and the group returned to the Nest. With the gentle patience of a peaceful dove, Scarlett happily let her friends go before her. But now it was her turn.

"Let us continue the journey," Dream Weaver said. "You have witnessed the path your friends have walked, and now the time has come for you, Scarlett. Does your heart feel ready to speak its voice?"

"I suppose I am as ready as I am going to be."

Scarlett gently set down a drawing of her family that her daughter drew when she was two.

Everyone smiled as this item perfectly embodied their friend.

"Wonderful. Stay in the present moment, and let the thoughts and visions come to you. Do not push or chase them. Simply share what you are shown."

Scarlett brushed away her worries and took a calming breath to ground herself. "I see something," she said with surprise.

> I am young, maybe four or five. I should preface this by telling you that I never got in trouble. My parents disciplined my older brother all the time. But not me. I was very well-behaved.
>
> We are about to meet my grandparents at a restaurant for dinner, and my family is waiting for me to get ready. When I finally come downstairs, I can see that my father is annoyed. He doesn't exactly yell, but I can tell he is frustrated when he abruptly says, "Let's go." Even now, I feel so bad I upset him. I burst into tears and crawl under the kitchen table.
>
> Since then, I don't think I've ever been late again.

"I can vouch for that," Carter said. "I have never seen Scarlett late for anything."

"Perhaps we will revisit why you changed your behavior as we progress. For now, return to your breath and allow whatever wishes to come forth to reveal itself," Dream Weaver said.

Scarlett took a deep breath and was ready to share. "It's like I'm right there."

> I'm nine years old and sitting at the same table I just mentioned. My father tells my brother and me that we're heading to the mountains instead of the

beach for our annual summer vacation. The news devastates me.

We've gone to the beach every summer of my life. I have pictures of myself as an infant sitting on my mother's lap under a beach umbrella. In the summer, we go to the beach. It's what we do. I am miserable for the next few weeks, but I don't want to complain, so I never mention it to my parents.

The thing is, the trip was wonderful. We went hiking and I caught my first fish. We watched the sunset over the mountains. Each night, we made a campfire and roasted marshmallows. Everything about it was magical.

I begged my parents to go back the next year.

"Ya see, change is good," Ian joked.

"Sometimes," Scarlett said. "But not always."

"Let's continue," Dream Weaver said. The visions were coming quickly now.

Some time has passed and I'm playing soccer. You guys probably didn't know that I played. It was just for one year, and here's why...

Apparently, soccer wasn't for me. The other girls had been playing for several years, so they had all the foundational skills. I'm watching the coach pull me aside to explain how to do the most basic practice drill, and it makes me look bad. I feel so embarrassed.

"Wait a sec," Dawn said. "It sounds like she was trying to help you. She didn't correct you in front of anyone else, which is a major no-no. Or, so I've been told."

"I guess that's one way to look at it. Anyway, it was clear that I wasn't good enough. I only played one season, and I was done."

"Sounds like you held onto that for quite a while," Dream Weaver said.

"I did because it hurt my feelings," Scarlett explained.

Dream Weaver reached across the circle and placed her hand on Scarlett's. "This is a safe space, and you are among friends. Take a few deep breaths and re-center yourself. Then, proceed when you are ready."

Scarlett steadied herself and brought forth another story.

Do you all remember my high school friend Dee?

Shortly after we met, someone asked her on a date and she complained that she had nothing to wear. We're about the same size, so I offer to lend her a sundress with a floral design. I loved that dress.

Dee is not the most cautious person I've ever met, and I thought about that when I gave her the dress. She promised to be careful. You can imagine what happens next. They go out for pizza, and she accidentally drops a blob of sauce on the dress.

I know accidents happen, but I am very upset. Without thinking, I call out her name and say a few choice words. For several days, I think I've lost my new friend. She ends up apologizing and we make up.

"Hold on," Dawn said. "She ruined *your* dress, and you thought she was mad at you?"

"Well, yeah. I yelled at her."

"Did you raise your voice?" Dawn asked.

"Not exactly."

"And she borrowed *your* dress and ruined it?"

"Yeah."

"Tell me again why you think she was mad at you," Dawn requested.

"We got into a fight and…"

"I'm not seeing the conflict here," Dawn interjected. "You were upset, and you showed emotions."

"It felt like we had an argument. And I was worried that she would hold it against me."

"Did she?" Ian asked.

"Well, no…" Scarlett replied. "But that's how friendships end. You fight, and people go their separate ways."

"If that's the rule," Dawn shrugged, "I'm in big trouble. If I were you, I would have been mad and told her so."

"Well, I don't like conflict. You all know that," Scarlett said.

Dream Weaver thanked the group for their candor and asked Scarlett to continue.

Ahhhh, here we go. This was a doozie. Dawn, I can already tell you that you will not be happy with me for this one.

I'm in high school, and my friends and I are planning on going to a music festival for the weekend. My neighbors, who I occasionally dog sit for, are going away for the weekend for their daughter's wedding, and they need someone to watch their dog. Their regular dog sitter can't do it, so they're stuck. I feel bad, so I agree to help.

"So, you missed the concert?" Ian asked.

"Oh, it gets worse. I discovered that their regular dog sitter couldn't do it because she attended the same concert I missed. I was so mad."

"That's horrible," Ian said. "I would have been so angry."

"In the dog sitter's defense, he didn't know I was planning on going to the concert."

"Why didn't you just say no?" Dawn asked.

"I guess I could have. But it was their daughter's wedding, and they needed help."

"You care deeply about those around you," said Dream Weaver. "I imagine we will return to this theme later. But right now, the stones are calling to the Fire Keeper. When we return, we will turn our gaze to the experiences that unfolded further along on your journey."

Reflections on the Level 1 Dove

At the first stage of development, Doves carry a deep fear of disappointing the most important people in their lives. After Scarlett made her family late for dinner, she was devastated when she sensed her father's frustration. The Dove's craving for harmony and approval makes them highly sensitive to the opinions of those around them. They naturally pick up on people's emotions, making them patient and empathetic listeners.

However, at the Unevolved State, Doves can take things personally and internalize the feelings of others. They may become overwhelmed by the emotional atmosphere in a room and struggle to differentiate between their feelings and everyone else's. If someone is upset, for example, they'll feel upset as a result. To avoid that discomfort, they'll go to great lengths to avoid any conflict that could lead anyone to feel upset. Notice how Scarlett said that she has never been late again. Just one experience of upsetting her father changed her behavior for a lifetime.

When Scarlett's vacation destination changed, we witnessed how crucial stability is in the life of the Level 1 Dove. For Scarlett, familiar patterns were a source of comfort and safety in an unpredictable world. These routines minimize uncertainties and the stress of surprises. The sudden change in plans forced Scarlett to confront the discomfort of the unknown, stirring feelings of anxiety and insecurity that she often preferred to avoid.

Doves are wired to seek consistency. In the DISC model, the S representing the Dove style has been represented by words such as *Steadiness*, *Stability*, and *Status Quo*. Those words convey the essence of the Dove at this stage.

PIQ1 Doves build long-lasting friendships and remain loyal, sometimes at their own expense. That devotion extends beyond people to brand loyalty—a Charmin Dove probably won't buy Cottonelle, even if it's less expensive. Doves tend to rotate a few standard meals at home and in restaurants. They like what they like, and they stick to it.

Notice how Scarlett reacted towards her parents when they made the switch from beach to mountains. Instead of addressing the issue directly, she responded in a passive-aggressive manner, letting her frustration simmer just below the surface. She might have made subtle comments, which hinted at her dissatisfaction without openly expressing her feelings. This behavior is characteristic of unevolved Doves, who often struggle to convey their emotions candidly, fearing that confrontation could lead to conflict or disapproval.

Similarly, when Scarlett received constructive feedback from her soccer coach, she internalized the advice as criticism. She then withdrew and felt inadequate. The feedback negatively affected her self-esteem.

Once again, the PIQ1 Dove's heightened sensitivity can lead them to perceive even well-intentioned remarks as a negative reflection of their worth, igniting feelings of inadequacy. Instead of viewing feedback as a valuable tool for improvement, Doves at this level may internalize it as a sign that they have let others down, intensifying their fear of disappointing those around them.

In defense, they may withdraw rather than constructively embrace the feedback as an opportunity to improve.

When Scarlett's friend ruined her dress, she felt like she was engaging in conflict. Unevolved Doves approach disagreements with great caution, as they are deeply averse to confrontation and disruption of harmony. From the Dove's perspective, conflict can destroy relationships, as Scarlett feared. Their natural inclination is to avoid tension, often seeking to smooth things over rather than address issues head-on. In times of disagreement, they may agree to solutions that don't necessarily align with their own desires simply to restore peace and prevent further discord. This leaves issues unresolved and can create a build-up of resentment.

In addition, Doves at PIQ1 can be people-pleasers who subjugate their wants to those of others. The Dove's self-esteem is wrapped up in their belief that they are only worthy if they serve those in need. We saw this when Scarlett missed the concert to help a neighbor. Level 1 Doves believe that failing to be supportive will lead to judgment or disapproval. So, they may take on too much or agree to things they don't want to do.

The Level 2 Dove

The Fire Keeper exchanged the cooled stones for fresh, heated ones and gently poured the sacred water over them. Exiting the Nest, he bowed his head slowly to Dream Weaver, who thanked him with a slight nod.

The group returned to their seats in the Nest and Dream Weaver spoke. "Step forward along the river of time. See what appears."

Before long, Scarlett's next memory came into view. "Okay, promise you won't tease me about this one."

Ian smiled. "I will try my best."

"Remember that old clunker I had when I started driving?"

"The one where your side mirror was held on by duct tape? How could we forget?" said Carter.

"Well, I don't think I told you what happened when it died."

I talked to friends and coworkers to see what cars they like, and several of them pointed me to the same car and a specific dealership. So, I went to check it out.

I arrived late in the day and by the time I was ready to take a test drive, the dealership was getting ready to close. The salesperson was very gracious and tells me I can take the car home and drive it around that night to see what I think. Then, I can bring it back the next morning, and we can talk. After a short drive, I realized I don't like it. That means I had to return to the nice salesperson and tell him I didn't want it.

"Why was that a problem?" Dawn asked.

"He was so friendly and helpful, how could I say no?"

"You just say no."

"If only it were that simple."

"What did you do?" Carter asked.

"Well, you know the car I picked you up in at the airport the last time you visited?"

Dawn's face froze. "You didn't?!?"

"I'm not proud of it," Scarlett admitted. "But I have to say, I ended up liking the car. I might even replace it with a newer model."

"You bought the car because you didn't want to let the salesperson down?" Dawn asked. She placed her hand on her forehead as if nursing a headache.

"This sounds like a topic to revisit on your vision quest. But right now, let's all take a deep breath and return to the stillness within," Dream Weaver gently suggested.

With the newly recharged stones, the visions came quickly.

I am at a meeting with my HR team, and we are trying to solve a controversial issue. A lot of our employees want to work remotely—not just from home, but from wherever they choose. Our CEO really doesn't want to make the change. Our CFO is concerned about the cost and tax implications. We want to find some middle ground, but the conversation gets quite contentious.

The first thing I do is calm everyone down. We aren't going to accomplish anything in such a heated discussion. Essentially, I suggest we take a break to settle down. The problem is, we never get back to it.

So, we didn't make any changes.

"That must have gone over well," Dawn noted.

"It didn't. Some people quit over our inaction. I suppose you can't please everyone," Scarlett sighed.

"If that were me," Dawn said, "I would have just made a decision and let the chips fall where they may."

"Oh, they fell," said Scarlett. She shrugged as if there was nothing she could have done.

"In retrospect, did your actions serve you and the team?" Dream Weaver asked.

"Not really, but I was glad I could minimize group conflict."

"I see," Dream Weaver replied. "Let's come back to this later."

Ahhhh, here's one that still bothers me.

I've always felt that honoring people on their birthday is the right thing to do. When I realized nobody was doing this at work, I take it upon myself to get a cake and a card for my team members on their special day. I pass the card around and we all write a personal message, then call the person to someone's office and sing them happy birthday.

I did this for a full year and felt like everyone sincerely appreciates it. But when my birthday rolls around, nobody celebrates me. There is no card. No cake.

Nobody singing me happy birthday. I think they feel bad about it, but the following year, they forget again!

After two years of buying cards and cakes, you would think *someone* would step up. So, the third year, I buy myself a cake and invite everyone to the conference room. I figured that accomplished two things: One, they celebrate my birthday, and two, I make them realize they should be more thoughtful and remember my birthday!

"Did you ever tell them that this bothered you?" Dawn asked.

"No. But they got the message," Scarlett replied.

"Did they?" Dawn asked.

"I guess we'll see on my next birthday."

Dream Weaver thanked Scarlett for sharing her birthday story and invited her to speak of a time when she embraced her true spirit.

Scarlett thought about it, then began.

My son is in fourth grade and I'm watching him at a music recital for his elementary school. It is adorable. The kids are wonderful, except maybe the violin players. That hurts my ears. Anyway, my son has been selected to perform a recorder solo. He has been practicing for weeks. In the printed program, I see that he is next; I'm both excited and nervous for him. Then, to my horror, the music teacher skips him and goes right to the next person.

I cannot let that stand. I walk straight down the center aisle and with everyone looking at me, I whisper in the music teacher's ear that she's forgotten my son.

She felt horrible and immediately called him next.

"You go, girl!" Ian cheered.

"I couldn't let them forget him. He worked so hard."

"It is a sacred honor to defend a child," Dream Weaver said.

"Thank you. I felt pretty good about myself."

"As you should," said Dream Weaver. "I sense there is one more story that wishes to be shared. If so, speak when it comes."

This is one you are all familiar with. When I was in college, I joined a community service club. I've always felt it's important to give back to the world.

One day in the heart of winter, I was walking to class and see a homeless man sitting in the cold without gloves. It really upset me. I worked with the club to create the Warm Hands program, where we collected and distributed gloves to the homeless.

"Scarlett is selling herself short. She came up with the idea and organized the first glove drive. That program still exists today. She's made a real difference," said Ian.

"I appreciate that," Scarlett said. "But a lot of people helped to make it happen."

"Yes," said Dawn. "But *you* were instrumental."

Not wanting to disagree with her friend, Scarlett let it go. She felt genuine pride in her accomplishments and gratitude for those who had lent their support. Above all, she found fulfillment in knowing she was positively impacting the world.

"This is a good place to pause and let the Fire Keeper tend to the stones. When we return, we will turn our eyes to Scarlett's path ahead."

Reflections on the Level 2 Dove

At Level 2, Doves demonstrate their style's strengths and challenges. One of the most significant challenges for PIQ2 Doves is getting comfortable saying no. Scarlett test drove a new car and didn't like it, but bought it anyway because that was less uncomfortable than saying no. That may be an extreme case for Level 2 Doves, but the underlying theme can be present throughout a Dove's life at this level.

Second-level Doves struggle with saying no because they have a deep-rooted longing to maintain harmony and avoid conflict. They are highly attuned to the physical and emotional needs of others, and consequently, they don't want to upset anyone.

On one hand, this makes Doves incredibly helpful and supportive. On the other hand, they may agree to inconvenient or burdensome requests, fearing that saying no could lead to disappointment or tension.

The PIQ2 Dove's fear of letting people down can cause them to neglect or deprioritize their own desires. Because they equate saying no with creating disharmony, they struggle to set boundaries, leading to a cycle of self-sacrifice, emotional exhaustion, and eventually, burnout and resentment. Doves may become overwhelmed by the demands placed upon them, yet still hesitate to speak up for themselves or assert their limits. Unable to meet the expectations they've taken on, the Dove may feel trapped and powerless to do anything about it.

Doves are natural peacekeepers who often go out of their way to mediate disputes and smooth over tensions to avoid uncomfortable confrontations. In the case of the remote work policy, Scarlett minimized conflict in the name of harmony, leaving the issue unresolved. In team situations, Doves may hold back their opinions if they believe they could spark conflict.

Level 2 Doves might even agree to decisions they don't fully support, if only to avoid rocking the boat. While their intentions are rooted in a yearning for unity, this conflict-avoidant approach can sometimes prevent the team from addressing significant concerns.

As Doves evolve, they recognize that healthy conflict is a natural part of growth and problem-solving. When they learn to embrace open, constructive dialogue, they help create a team environment that is both stable and dynamic, where all voices are heard. In personal relationships, happy couples know how to argue. Doves understand that disagreements happen, and they know how to work through them without creating resentment.

Notice how Scarlett handled her disappointment that no one celebrated her birthday. She never expressed her dissatisfaction and never said she wanted someone on her team to buy her a cake and a card. Instead, she hosted a birthday celebration for herself to indirectly express her needs. To Scarlett, the intended message was clear. To her team, maybe not. Scarlett might get even angrier if they don't throw a celebration for her next year.

In that same birthday story, we also witnessed the PIQ2 Dove as the martyr. At this stage of Personality Intelligence, Doves have a deep urge to be supportive, which can lead them to take on responsibilities that are not their own—like throwing every single birthday celebration. While this selflessness stems from genuinely wanting to help, it can result in a one-sided dynamic where Doves feel overwhelmed by the weight of their commitments and resentful that the support isn't reciprocated. This can provoke passive-aggressive behaviors, like buying one's own birthday cake.

Ultimately, it is crucial for Doves to recognize the importance of self-care and to set healthy boundaries. By learning to express themselves and advocate for their well-being, they can step out of the martyr role and build more balanced, fulfilling relationships where both their desires and contributions are valued.

Although Level 2 Doves may find it challenging to advocate for themselves, they may feel more comfortable standing up for those who they care deeply about. This was visible when Scarlett fought for her son to play his recorder solo at the concert. As Doves evolve, they gain command and advocate for themselves as well.

Doves frequently downplay their own contributions, preferring to share the credit for their work with the rest of the team. Scarlett demonstrates this when she minimized her role in developing the Warm Hands program. While it's thoughtful to credit everyone for their contributions, Doves often can take this selflessness too far by diminishing their own impact.

That story also illustrates how Doves channel their compassion into making an impact. PIQ2 Doves proactively think of those around them and address the unstated before it is voiced. Their sensitivity to the feelings and circumstances of others drives them to action, whether through small gestures of kindness or more significant initiatives. Their nurturing, uplifting spirit can be a powerful force for good.

The Level 3 Dove

Once everyone found their place in the Nest, Dream Weaver spoke. "You all understand the way of the circle. The time has come to share with Scarlett the wisdom to balance her innate talents. Speak freely and share your thoughts when your heart calls you."

"I'll kick us off," Dawn said. "Scarlett is incredibly helpful. Whenever anyone needs help, she drops everything and is there for you."

"How does that sometimes work against you?" Dream Weaver asked Scarlett.

"Sometimes I drop things that shouldn't be dropped, as I put other people before myself."

"To walk in balance, you must find the middle path, where you honor both your spirit and that of others," Dream Weaver advised. "What else?"

"Many of Scarlett's stories seem to be centered on seeking harmony. I've always loved that about her," Ian said.

"And the opposite," Dawn began, "would be to get comfortable with rocking the boat and saying the things that have to be said, even if they may ruffle some feathers."

"Keep going," encouraged Dream Weaver.

"I would add that Scarlett is incredibly loyal," Carter said.

"Where do you see this reflected in her life?" Dream Weaver asked.

"Everywhere!" exclaimed Ian.

"Like where?" Scarlett asked.

"Of course, you are loyal to your friends. I would trust you with my life. But you are also loyal to every product you use. I'll bet you've been using the same shampoo since the day I met you."

"Yeah, because I like it."

"How about soap?"

"Yeah," she said sheepishly.

"Toothpaste?"

"Okay, I see your point," Scarlett conceded. "So, how do I bring that into balance?"

"I'm not suggesting you become less loyal to people. But with products and the things you do, maybe you could switch things up now and then and see what happens."

"I can do that. Keep it going. I appreciate this."

"Playing off of loyalty, Scarlett will fight to the death for someone she loves," Dawn said.

"I would love to see her fight equally hard for herself," Carter said.

"I hear you. I will pay attention to that."

"Adding to what Carter shared, I would say she is conflict-averse," Dawn said. "That serves her because she doesn't get into arguments. But if she gets comfortable with conflict, she could resolve issues more quickly," Dawn suggested.

"Just kill me now," Scarlett joked. "Are you suggesting that I get into more arguments?"

"That's exactly what I'm saying. Give me a call. I'll help you with this one," Dawn offered.

"I'm sure life will present plenty of opportunities for conflict," Dream Weaver said, amused by the thought of Dawn and Scarlett practicing arguments.

"I, for one, would add that Scarlett is incredibly giving and caring," Ian said.

Scarlett nodded thoughtfully. "I understand how to bring balance to this. I've been told I can be a bit overbearing at times. I'll offer to help someone, and even if they say no, I assume they want it but feel uneasy asking. So, I end up pushing my help on them."

Dream Weaver looked kindly at Scarlett. "These words carry great wisdom. Do you feel these teachings are enough to assist you on your journey ahead?"

"I think they are enough for a lifetime," Scarlett said.

"And so, it is written. Before we adjourn, a special guest will join us after taking a short break. Stretch your legs and we will begin shortly."

Reflections on the Level 3 Dove

William Marston described Doves as people who view the world as welcoming and friendly. However, they often perceive themselves as having less power or influence than the world around them. This perception drives their desire for approval and acceptance, especially within groups. They tend to avoid conflict and strive to maintain peace and harmony.

While the Dove's natural inclination is to nurture and protect, they must learn to channel that same compassion inward, ensuring they are valued and respected. Level 3 Doves stand up for themselves with the same ferocity and dedication they channel when defending others.

At PIQ3, Doves move beyond the desire to be liked by everyone. They recognize that conflict is sometimes necessary to resolve issues. They also recognize that saying no to others sometimes means saying yes to themselves. They know they must manage their time, or someone else will. This allows them to set healthy boundaries and cultivate a more profound sense of self-respect and balance.

Doves who have mastered their style offer support freely without expecting anything in return. They give because it is their choice. It doesn't matter if others reciprocate or express thanks; their actions come without strings attached.

Master Doves are not bound by tradition or routine. They remain open to new experiences and possibilities. While they may find comfort in familiar surroundings, they also find fulfillment in exploring the unknown and embracing the new.

At this level, Doves understand the limits of the support they can and should offer. While the Dove's nurturing nature drives them to help and uplift those around them, they respect that sometimes people have to learn the hard way, and allowing for that is an act of compassion.

At this highest level of Personality Intelligence, Doves willingly make tough decisions. Gentle but firm, they do what must be done with conviction. They show up for themselves and others. And while they reveal a humble exterior, they feel empowered and believe in themselves.

Real-Life Level 3 Doves

Selena Gomez

At the 2025 Golden Globe Awards, actress, singer, producer, and businesswoman Selena Gomez was honored for a role that has raised enormous controversy. That's a place no Dove likes to be, but Gomez's handling of the situation is a masterclass in being a Level 3 Dove.

In the movie *Emilia Pérez*, Gomez plays Jessi Del Monte, wife of a Mexican cartel leader who undergoes gender-affirming surgery. On a podcast, Mexican actor and comedian Eugenio Derbez critiqued Gomez for playing a character fluent in Spanish despite not being fluent herself. Gomez stood up for herself, with balance: "I understand where you are coming from. I'm sorry, I did the best I could with the time I was given," she wrote in the comment section of a TikTok video showing that segment—a low-key response for someone with 423 million followers on

Instagram. "Doesn't take away from how much work and heart I put into this movie."

In response, the critical actor gave an emotional apology, lauding Gomez for her "kind heart." That is a Level 3 Dove in action. They don't play martyr or victim like lower-level Doves. They don't tell their critics they're right, just to avoid conflict. They combine the Dove's self-reflectiveness with Eagle assertiveness to deliver a response so good that their antagonist feels bad.

Just to get roles in serious movies, like *Emilia Pérez,* Gomez has had to use Level 3 Dove skills. When most A-list celebrities audition for a role, they want the casting team and director to know *they* are putting their hat in the ring. Not Gomez. She doesn't want to be pre-judged for her age or Disney legacy or any other extraneous baggage, so she submits tapes anonymously. Or, she has her managers put her up for auditions as "a client," not as *the* Selena Gomez.

Why? She knows Hollywood sees her as "soft-spoken and the underdog character," she says in an interview with *Hollywood Reporter.* Dove indeed. But she doesn't want to be rejected automatically, just because of this reputation. "I'll put myself in that room, no matter what it takes," she says. PIQ1 Doves take rejection poorly; PIQ2 Doves accept it; PIQ3 Doves take bold measures to prevent rejection and then, don't internalize it and allow it to affect their self-esteem. The French director who casted Gomez in *Emilia Pérez* had no idea until afterwards that she was such a big name, and that was by her design.

Gomez also shows how a Master Dove can turn a sensitive, difficult issue into a source of strength. When Gomez canceled a music tour in 2016, citing her struggle with lupus and its impact on her mental health, critics accused her of playing victim. When doctors determined that she had bipolar disorder, many people cautioned her against revealing it, thinking that doing so would harm her career. Gomez refused to hide: "It was terrifying for me to let people inside my world that way, but I was doing it because I felt like maybe this would help someone, and that's what I care about."

Speaking up bravely was only the start for Gomez. She then founded Rare Beauty, a cosmetics brand that "is breaking down unrealistic standards of perfection" and donates a portion of sales to mental health causes. Its success has made Gomez a billionaire. She's also a co-founder of the online platform Wondermind, "The World's First Mental Health Ecosystem."

Gomez demonstrates how a Level 3 Dove embraces Eagle boldness and independence to thrive, especially in moments of conflict and vulnerability. She is powerful because of, not in spite of, her humility and compassion.

Keanu Reeves

If you Google "nicest guy in Hollywood," actor Keanu Reeves will appear in almost all of the lists in the search results. His Dove nature has made him renowned not just for his kindness, but also for his acts of selflessness and generosity that exemplify the Level 3 Dove. Reeves is a Mr. Nice Guy who channels Eagle traits in his acting roles and daily life.

Best known as the lead in two movie franchises—*The Matrix* and *John Wick*—Reeves found his sweet spot playing understated, soft-spoken characters who, pushed too far by injustice, take extreme action. Both franchises use the story arc of a Dove who, reluctantly, must leave a comfortable life and embody the relentless determination of an Eagle to do what is right. In essence, they show the making of a Master Dove.

In *The Matrix,* Reeves' character, Neo, leads a rebellion against robots that have conquered the "real world" and enslaved human beings in a virtual reality. He fights as a messianic figure of prophecy.

As John Wick, Reeves plays a grieving widower whose parting gift from his late wife, a dog, is murdered by criminals. Wick, a retired assassin who left the business to be with his wife, exacts revenge for his dog and ultimately revolts against the shadowy leaders of the assassin world, putting loyalty to his friends and values over obedience to the powers that be. It's Dove intention with Eagle execution. In other words, the Master Level 3.

Of course, actors act. Who they are in movies isn't necessarily who they are in real life. Reeves, however, seems to be a PIQ3 Dove both on and off screen.

Reportedly, Reeves took a pay cut on *The Matrix* to ensure that the production could afford proper special effects and costumes while still paying the crew good wages. Following the film's box office success, he paid seventy-five million dollars in bonuses to crew who don't normally get to share in the backend profits. He has also gifted Harley-Davidson motorcycles and Rolex watches to stunt people in gratitude for the risks they took on the sets of both *The Matrix* and *John Wick* movies.

His selflessness extends to strangers as well. There are images and videos of Reeves playing catch with two young fans, giving up his seat on public transit for a woman in need, and having a meal and conversation with a homeless man. While some Dove stars avoid the spotlight, Reeves puts empathy and compassion for others first. He doesn't want to make a scene, but if thoughtful action leads to attention, so be it.

A Level 1 or 2 Dove is usually kind to people too, but a Level 3 Dove acts from the heart in big, Eagle-scale ways. Unlike an Eagle, though, Reeves feels no need to talk about these acts of kindness. His private foundation, for example, makes donations to children's hospitals and cancer research anonymously. There are no ceremonies, no plaques, and no hospital wings named after him.

If one sentence perfectly embodies Reeves' master Dove, it came during an interview on *The Late Show with Stephen Colbert*. When Colbert asked what happens when we die, Reeves responded, "I know that the ones who love us will miss us." He left Colbert speechless. Pure empathy. Pure selflessness. Pure Dove.

Reeves' compassion, generosity, and humility are Dove in nature. By adding Eagle boldness and assertiveness, he rises to Level 3 Dove. That has endeared him to fans, costars, crew, and the media alike.

Chapter 14:
The Chameleon

The Chameleon at Levels 1 and 4

The Fire Keeper readied the Nest while the four friends took a short walk to stretch their legs. Upon their return, they found the Fire Keeper seated beside Dream Weaver. Once everyone settled in, Dream Weaver began to speak. "You have all met my brother, the Fire Keeper. I have asked him to share with you who he was in his early years and the journey he took to become the person he is today. Things will move swiftly, so keep your mind sharp and your ears open."

Fire Keeper reached into his pocket and removed a hand-carved chameleon, which he placed on the floor in front of him. After a long, slow inhale and exhale, Fire Keeper's words started flowing almost immediately.

When I was a young sprout, I was too much for my parents and teachers to handle. I had no focus. I asked more questions than anyone wanted to answer. The fire within me was strong, and I took dangerous risks. I thought I was above my elders and peers. I had to know everything about everything. My emotions ran deep and at the same time, I had the boundless energy of a litter of puppies.

Nobody knew what to do with me. As people today might say, I was "a lot."

"I took a lot of unnecessary risks when I was young," added Dawn.

"I understand the part about asking a lot of questions," Carter said.

"I always cared about how others feel. Maybe too much so," Scarlett said.

"And one of my teachers once called me an octopus on roller skates. So I get what it's like to be a playful puppy," Ian said.

"I want to be very clear," said Fire Keeper. "I carried all those traits in their most intense form."

"None among us are born with mastery," offered Dream Weaver. "Through many seasons, Fire Keeper learned to tame the wild flames within. Once like a forest fire, his spirit now burns with purpose and wisdom. He learned to master his own flame."

Dream Weaver met her brother's eyes, and with a simple glance and nod, she silently asked him to paint the picture of what it means to be a master in action.

I am not just a Fire Keeper. By day, I lead a large department at a local manufacturing firm.

We were about to change a key process, and the time had come to share it with the staff. We had a diverse group of employees, and I wanted to touch each of their hearts. I had to find the voice within myself to bridge my spirit to theirs.

I began by sharing the larger vision, the purpose that guided us. I spoke of how this new way would bolster our company and bring success to our people.

Then, with a heart full of excitement, I shared my joy for this new way. I spoke with enthusiasm, showing how this path would be swifter, simpler, and stronger than the one we had walked before.

I understood that this new path would bring change, which can feel unsettling for some. I assured my people that we would walk alongside them, ready to listen to their questions and concerns. I spoke of how this new way would serve us better, bringing stability to those within our circle and those we serve.

Finally, I shared the details of our journey ahead. I spoke of the steps we would follow, how this new way would unfold, and the reasons behind it. I laid out the timeline for our path and how we would embrace this change gradually. Then, I opened my heart to their questions, ready to listen and guide.

The four friends were now in awe of Fire Keeper. "I would have liked how you started if I were there," Dawn said. "Give me the goal and the expected impact, and I am good."

"You had me at 'excitement,'" Ian said. "I don't need lots of details. Just tell me how awesome it is and I'm with you!"

"Your approach would have made me feel comfortable," Scarlett said. "I would have appreciated that you understood my concerns about change and pledged to be there for me.

"I wish everyone would provide all the details and the logic behind changes like you did," Carter said. "Projects would go so much smoother if that were the case."

The Fire Keeper offered a gentle bow to everyone in the Nest. He then rose and left the four friends with Dream Weaver.

"That was amazing," Ian said. "Somehow, he appealed to all of us."

Dream Weaver nodded in agreement. "Like water that takes the form of any vessel, he is a shapeshifter. He can be strong or gentle, full of life or still as the quiet stream. He walks between the worlds of vision from the sky above and the details that ground us, always flowing with the spirit."

The ceremony concluded with expressions of gratitude. Before they left, they worked together to disassemble the Nest and clean the area. In the spirit of leaving the space as they found it, they returned all of the building materials to nature.

The four friends felt a profound sense of peace and fullness of being. They had journeyed through the heat, faced their fears, and emerged on the other side, renewed and invigorated.

Upon returning to the parking area, Dream Weaver gave each of them a cup of cool water, which they drank slowly, savoring the sensation of cleansing them from within. Before they left, she said, "You have walked the path of the seeker. May you carry the lessons of the Nest with you always."

They nodded as a feeling of deep gratitude swept over them. Throughout the evening, they talked about how they felt lighter, clearer, and more connected to themselves, each other, and the world around them. They returned home, not as different people, but as more authentic versions of themselves. They knew this experience would always be a part of them.

The Chameleon in the Shadow

When we think of Chameleons, we envision them as being at Level 4, the highest stage of Personality Intelligence. But there is also a Level 1 version of the Chameleon. Remember the Too-Much People? They are back and bigger than ever.

At the beginning of the Fire Keeper's story, he described himself as being at the Unevolved State of each style. He was reckless like a Level 1 Eagle and overly inquisitive like a first-stage Owl. His energy overwhelmed others like a Parrot, while his strong Dove emotions were too much to handle.

On one hand, since he was tapping into all four styles, one might call him a Chameleon. But since he was overusing every style, he was a Too-Much Chameleon functioning at Level 1.

For most, the path to becoming the Chameleon is to master one's style and then master all of them. We saw this through Dawn, Ian, Scarlett, and Carter's stories. Each of them started at Level 1, lacking awareness of their style. They then progressed to Level 2, where they began to employ the strengths and challenges of their style. From there, we saw what they would look like if they balanced their traits and mastered their styles.

However, a small but intense subset of the population follows a different path to Chameleon status. These individuals embody all four styles at the outset, like Fire Keeper. He expressed all four styles from a young age, each was amplified so sharply that he exhibited all their challenges. His elders didn't know what to do with him.

Since Too-Much Chameleons have unique access to all styles, they are indeed on the path to becoming a master of all styles. To get there, they must temper the intensity of each style and hone the core strengths of all four.

The Chameleon in the Light

The Fire Keeper's story about how he communicated to a group using all four styles demonstrates that he left the Chameleon's shadow and entered its light. Those at Level 4 have mastered Personality Intelligence and are able to adapt in real-time. Rather than impose their style, Chameleons authentically reflect the style of those they interact with, modifying their tone, body language, and communication to meet the moment.

While anyone can display any style, operating outside of our natural tendencies tends to be draining. In contrast, individuals at PIQ4 seamlessly adjust their approach to fit each situation without expending unnecessary energy. Their effortless adaptability not only preserves their vitality but also enhances their interactions, allowing them to remain effective and engaged.

With their high level of emotional awareness and dynamic social skills, Chameleons deeply understand and resonate with the experiences of others. They can lead and navigate complex communities while making everyone feel heard and valued.

High-level Chameleons can connect with diverse styles simultaneously, meeting everyone's needs. The Fire Keeper communicated with Eagles when he conveyed the big picture, with Parrots as he infused excitement, with Doves when he showed kindness, and with Owls when he provided detailed information. This adaptability is the key to making everyone feel included and understood.

Chameleons cultivate meaningful relationships and are highly effective in their chosen careers. Ultimately, their flexibility leads to more fulfilling personal and professional lives.

Chameleons Respond to Intention

We tend to judge ourselves by our intentions but others by their behavior. Why do we excuse our own missteps but not extend this leniency to others? Because we have access to our intentions, but not to the intentions of others. We only hear their words and see their outward behaviors and guess their motivations from those signals.

But Chameleons who understand all the styles have a window into the intentions of others. They recognize the fears and desires that drive people's intentions and don't get triggered by what is said or done.

When an Owl asks many questions after being presented with a new idea, people at lower levels of Personality Intelligence may assume the questions are meant to shoot down the idea. In fact, they may reflect the Owl's intent to minimize mistakes or problems. The questions have nothing to do with the idea or who presented it.

When an Eagle takes over and doesn't allow anyone else to play their part, it doesn't mean they lack trust in others. It means they fear not getting the desired results and believe only they can make it happen. Their actions have nothing to do with anyone else's competency.

When a Parrot shares the bright side of an upsetting situation, it doesn't mean they don't understand the pain. They are actually trying to alleviate it.

And when a Dove says they don't care where to have dinner, and suggests that someone else choose, it doesn't mean they don't have a preference; it means they feel driven to satisfy others before themselves.

Because Chameleons intimately understand the four styles, they can look beyond the words and actions of others and interpret what is happening through the lens of the underlying motivation.

That's how a Chameleon always seems to respond with empathy and exhibit a response that honors the underlying needs. Rather than feel triggered by words and actions, Chameleons use them to read and respond to situations with grace.

Chameleons at Level 4

We've discussed the skills and qualities that make Level 4 Chameleons successful in all walks of life and so capable of reinvention. Now, we will explore the lives of two individuals who have harnessed their Chameleon-like adaptability to thrive far beyond their initial career path.

Dwayne (The Rock) Johnson

Dwayne Johnson embodies all four styles. The Eagle can be seen in his career as a professional wrestler, where he radiated Eagle energy. He would take the microphone and command the ring. It's no surprise he rose to the top of the WWE, becoming one of the most iconic and successful superstars in wrestling history. As The Rock, he was a cocky, charismatic villain who skyrocketed in popularity. He won ten WWE world titles and dominated main event matches at WrestleMania, WWE's biggest stage.

Through his relentless ambition, he transitioned from a wrestler to become one of Hollywood's highest-paid actors. In his early roles, he was all Eagle. Whether in *Walking Tall* in 2004 or *The Rundown* in 2003, Johnson played characters who refused to back down, even when outnumbered or underestimated. His roles often involved taking on corrupt systems or tough enemies with unshakable Eagle confidence.

Later, Johnson let his inner Parrot shine in films like *Jumanji: Welcome to the Jungle* in 2017, where he was expressive and over-the-top. Johnson's characters increasingly focus on engaging the audience, not just defeating bad guys. Roles in movies like *Central Intelligence* in 2016 and *Red Notice* in 2021 show him as a lovable goofball who doesn't take himself too seriously. He's not just winning battles, he's winning hearts with his humor and warmth. He didn't just act in movies, *he lit them up*.

Dwayne Johnson candidly shares his personal struggles and vulnerabilities, offering heartfelt stories and advice that resonate deeply. By speaking openly about mental health, he forges genuine connections and encourages others to seek the support they need. His Dove style also shines through in how he expresses gratitude, consistently remaining humble and appreciative of the fans who have supported him throughout his journey.

While speaking to an audience, he recalled a quote that has stayed with him since he was 15: "It's nice to be important, but it's more important to be nice." He carries those words with him as a guiding principle, woven into who he is.

Meanwhile, his highly disciplined approach to fitness, involving strict workouts and meal plans, shows his methodical Owl nature. His Owl style is also evident in his work as a producer and an entrepreneur, as he ensures that projects are executed with care and precision.

Like other Level 4 Chameleons, Dwayne Johnson has achieved remarkable success across a diverse range of fields, excelling in each of them.

Taylor Swift

Why are people of different ages, backgrounds, and cultures so passionate about musician Taylor Swift? Throughout her Eras Tour, many paid thousands of dollars per ticket to see her perform live. They even paid money to watch a film of her performing in concert, screened at their local movie theaters. Her biggest fans, "Swifties," are passionate not because she's the world's best singer or dancer—many will concede she isn't—rather, they gravitate to her versatile Chameleon personality that has something to offer everyone.

Swifties love the fact that no one can mess with Swift and get away with it. That's her Eagle side. A famous example is her beef with talent manager Scooter Braun. In 2019, Swift's former label, Big Machine Records, sold to Scooter Braun, giving him control over Swift's first six studio albums. He allegedly bullied Swift, preventing her from performing her own music. So, Swift re-recorded and re-released all six studio albums. In 2025, she purchased all the original masters, thus regaining licensing rights to all of her songs. She won the feud, igniting a movement among artists to retain or regain control over their music.

Swift's Parrot side shows up in predictable ways, with visually stunning sets, mesmerizing choreography, and memorable costumes, but it also shows up unexpectedly. When Swift performed at Gillette Stadium in Massachusetts in 2023 during her Eras Tour, rain damaged her piano before one of the shows. She didn't realize it until she sat down to play, so she improvised on the spot. She picked up her guitar and surprised the crowd by playing a song that she hadn't even practiced. The audience loved it. That's go-with-the-flow Parrot mastery.

On stage, Swift's Dove side comes out between songs, where she tells the stories and emotions behind each one. Fans gravitate toward that genuine, vulnerable way of making the music relatable and meaningful. And rather than stick with one charitable cause, Swift lets the needs of the moment guide her heart. She has given to disaster relief, to women who lost their partners to COVID-19, to pet rescues, to grieving police departments, to victims of shootings and terrorism, among other causes. She is also known to support fans in distress by contributing to their medical bills, rent, and student loans.

The Owl side of Taylor Swift is most visible in her complex, poetic songwriting. In fact, fans debate vigorously about what her lyrics mean. They also debate the "Easter eggs" hidden in music videos, album art, and lyrics. Usually, those kinds of debates only happen in literature and philosophy classes. It takes some Owl depth to write lyrics so complex and so interesting that people enjoy arguing about them.

Swift is the full Chameleon package—a master of Eagle, Parrot, Dove, and Owl traits. No wonder everyone can find something to love in her art.

Up Next

Level 4 individuals are few and far between, but if you encounter one, pay attention to everything they do! You are in the presence of a master. So, how can you achieve PIQ4 status and become a Chameleon? Let's go there now.

Part IV:
Increasing Your Personality Intelligence

Chapter 15:
How to Advance Levels

Now that you understand the styles at each of the four levels of Personality Intelligence, the next question is, how does one advance from one level to the next?

For some individuals, the progression is unconscious and happens slowly over time. As they age, they evolve. Sometimes, a defining event can cause them to shift. People also learn from books, videos, training programs, and coaches, as well as by adopting the behaviors of those they admire, such as parents, coworkers, or spiritual leaders.

Lifelong learners put in the time, energy, and effort to do the work. They actively seek ways to improve. The fact that you are reading this book puts you in that category.

If you want to advance to the next level of Personality Intelligence, do what lifelong learners do. Reflect on your talents and look for ways to improve. Let go of self-judgment, practice self-compassion, and accept yourself fully. Be curious, resilient, and mindful. Seek feedback to understand what you are projecting to the world. Then, be open to what you discover.

Look for ways and reasons to evolve, and you will find them.

Advancing from Level 1 to Level 2

If you are at PIQ1, reflect on the feedback you have consistently received throughout your life. Consider what your parents, friends, teachers, and managers have encouraged you to work on. There are probably common themes and patterns.

For example, a Parrot child might become injured after not considering the consequences of his actions. Later, as an adult, his manager might tell him to slow down and think things through before taking risks.

By contrast, an Owl child may not complete a test in school because she feels the need to double- and triple-check her work. As an adult, she may be told that things don't have to be perfect, and that she needs to speed up to be more productive in the workplace.

Pay careful attention to your relationships that fell apart. What conflicts emerged and why? Chances are, the same needs and fears created tension in different settings.

A Dove child may decide not to be friends with someone because that individual hurts their feelings. This same issue may repeat itself in adult relationships.

If you want to shift from Level 1 to Level 2, set big improvement goals and break them down into smaller, manageable steps. Then, take consistent action to achieve them. For example, pick a scenario that regularly creates conflict between you and a coworker. Visualize, in advance, how a Level 2 or 3 member of your style would handle it differently. Give it a shot.

For instance, if you are an Eagle and you find that impatience has been an issue for you, look for places that this issue manifests itself. In conversations, listen intently and don't fast forward the conversation to the action step. When making a decision, slow down and consider the implications of your actions. When replying to an email, make sure you answer all of the questions. And maybe throw in a, "I hope this finds you well" or "Have a great day." Look for opportunities to be more patient and work on them one at a time.

Recognize and celebrate your progress, no matter how small. Don't judge yourself when you slip back. That's only natural. Acknowledge the setback and commit to doing better next time.

Challenge yourself to take on progressively harder tasks. Push your boundaries, and you will grow faster. In whatever area you set improvement goals—giving feedback, listening deeply, being assertive, accepting mistakes, etc.—find a book or two that provides wisdom about that specific skill set. Read articles and watch videos. There is likely expert advice on how to grow in the exact area you have identified, and it's at your fingertips. Seek it. Absorb it. And do it.

It is said that we are the sum total of the people we hang out with. So, stop hanging out with individuals who pull you backward and spend more time with those who will help you grow. If you are at Level 1 and want to advance to Level 2, hang out with people of your style who are further down the path than you. Their skills will rub off on you.

Dedicate time for self-reflection. Examine your thoughts, emotions, and behaviors. Journaling can be an effective way to identify patterns and track progress. Use the following prompts to get started.

- When do I feel most confident and what contributes to that feeling?
- What limiting beliefs do I hold about myself and how can I challenge them?
- If I could give my younger self one piece of advice, what would it be?
- What emotions have I been feeling today and why?
- What is something I've been avoiding and why?
- What traits make me unique?
- What is my superpower?
- If I could instantly master any skill, what would it be and why?
- How have I grown in the past year?
- What is one thing I can celebrate about myself right now?

Finally, be open to change. Cultivate a mindset that is open to new experiences and perspectives and a new level of quality in your relationships. Embrace the idea that growth often requires stepping outside of your comfort zone and challenging your usual way of thinking. When you allow yourself to adapt, you create space for deeper connections, richer experiences, and more meaningful personal development.

Advancing from Level 2 to 3

If you have reached PIQ2, it's time to level up and master your style. But fair warning, very few people make this transition. Self-reflection is not easy or comfortable, and most people fail to commit to changing the behaviors that stand between them and PIQ3.

Anyone can earn a black belt in karate, yet few will even walk through the dojo door for the first time. They incorrectly believe they don't have the right body type or discipline or coordination or whatever, so they never try. They fail to realize that martial arts will develop what they lack. Self-limiting beliefs inhibit growth before it can begin. Let go of negative self-talk and replace it with words that encourage you.

We learn by modeling, so identify someone you believe has mastered your style and do your best to emulate them. This could be someone you know, a famous individual, or even a fictitious character from a television show, movie, or book. The key is to pick someone who shares your style so you can more easily visualize advancing within it and becoming an authentic version of yourself.

When making decisions, make it your mantra to ask yourself what that person would do. This is a tried-and-true strategy. You may have seen bracelets with the words, "What would Jesus do?" or "What would Buddha do?" In this case, find someone who exists in the Master State of your style and ask, "What would they do?"

You could also ask yourself, "If I were acting at the highest level of my style, how would I handle this situation?" Then, be silent. Listen for the answer and take your own advice.

As with shifting from Level 1 to Level 2, if you want to reach Level 3 of Personality Intelligence, find good teachers. As with Level 2, recall that we are the sum of the people we hang out with. So, hang out with people who are fountains, not drains. Removing individuals from our lives is challenging for a variety of reasons, but if you've ever had a toxic individual leave your life, it probably felt like you could breathe again after they left. Consciously get rid of those who push you backward on your Personality Intelligence journey, and if that's not possible, set clear boundaries.

Another way to master your style is to teach those around you what you have learned. My most significant learnings about my own style came from sharing the styles, and you can share them too. Offer the insights you have gained about yourself and the four styles.

In martial arts, *sensei* does not mean instructor, teacher, or master. It means "one who has come before." If you have walked the path of the styles longer than someone else, share your wisdom. You don't have to be a facilitator in a classroom or a speaker at a conference. If you are a parent, you are a teacher. If you are a human being, you have walked the path longer than many, and you are a teacher.

Another strategy for mastering Level 3 of Personality Intelligence is to accept your style's paradoxes. Recall what Dawn, Ian, Scarlett, and Carter learned in the Nest. Examine your greatest strengths and embrace their complement. Eagles can balance their big-picture vision by paying attention to the details. They can be candid and sensitive with their words and anticipate consequences before they take risks.

Parrots can rely on intuition while making calculated, data-driven decisions. They can display charisma and excitement and balance those with seriousness and focus. They can imagine the possibilities while maintaining a sense of realism.

Doves can embrace the dichotomies of humility and confidence. They can provide support while maintaining boundaries and focus on themselves while acting with empathy towards others.

Owls can plan while leaving room for spontaneity. They can make quality decisions, even when time is short, data is limited, and the details are innumerable.

Finally, individuals at Level 3 tend to display the behaviors of someone who seems to be enlightened, or at least highly fulfilled. Arriving there can be scary, as it is a radical departure from what we experience in our daily lives. Our culture and media are overflowing with Level 1 behavior because it makes for captivating stories.

To prepare for that, let go of ego and the opinions of others. Transcend the pursuit for approval and strive to connect with your true self. Live by higher principles of compassion, reliability, and integrity. Engage in acts of kindness and service, cultivate unity with the people you meet, practice radical acceptance of yourself and others, and allow for the grace of making mistakes. Cultivate inner peace by developing practices that help you stay calm and focused. Practice accepting life as it is, surrendering to the flow of existence, and letting go of resistance. Be the light.

Level 3 exists on the path before you. You just need to walk it.

Advancing from Level 3 to 4

If you've attained Level 3 of Personality Intelligence, you are on your way to Level 4. Now you have three more styles to master, or possibly two if you have a strong secondary style and have already mastered it.

The remaining styles will seem far more accessible now that you've gained self-esteem, self-awareness, and self-discipline through mastering your primary style. That said, the road to Level 4 presents a distinctly different challenge from Level 3.

While progressing towards style mastery (Level 3), the main challenge is to avoid overusing your primary style. When seeking to master Level 4, however, the challenge is to tap into all four styles and not underuse your lowest style. (If you've completed Take Flight Learning's *Taking Flight Profile*, this would be the lowest style on the graph.)

This is easier explained than done because we all become deeply rooted in our own natural style and come to rely heavily on the traits that have served us in the past. We've experienced success and comfort by playing to these innate abilities, so swapping them for less familiar behaviors becomes difficult. But to truly master all four styles, we must embrace the unique abilities that each one offers.

Mastering all four styles means recognizing when a different approach may be more effective. Like Sensei Tori in the sparring matches with his students, Chameleons adapt to the style best suited to the situation.

Being a Chameleon isn't about creating new personas. It's about activating existing ones that are less prominent. Remember, our brains are wired for all four styles. Find that wiring and light it up. The more you exhibit a behavior, the more hardwiring you lay down for that behavior, and the easier it becomes the next time it's required.

Additionally, mastering all four styles requires humility. It's not just about knowing each style's abilities but also recognizing your limitations and being open to the idea that other styles offer valuable perspectives and approaches.

Humility leads to flexibility, the essence of a Chameleon. Rather than always relying on what comes naturally to you, challenge yourself to view problems through the lens of a different style. For instance, if you naturally gravitate toward leading an Owl's planned and organized life, see what happens when you embrace the Parrot's go-with-the-flow way of being. Practicing flexibility will broaden your problem-solving toolkit.

With practice, you'll develop greater versatility and learn how to tap into the hidden strengths of the styles you may have overlooked. By intentionally exploring and practicing other styles, you will learn to be the Chameleon without thinking about it. Nothing can stand in your way if all the styles are at your command.

Release Imposter Syndrome

As you progress to a new level, unfamiliar behaviors may feel unnatural. New neural pathways need to form, and until these skills are well-ingrained, the behaviors might remain uncomfortable. During this adjustment phase, you may feel like you're faking it.

This sense of self-doubt is known as Imposter Syndrome, a psychological phenomenon where individuals question their abilities and fear being seen as a fraud, even though they have developed competence. You feel it most when you're on the cusp of a new level.

Individuals with Imposter Syndrome often credit their achievements to luck or outside factors, overlooking their own growth. To overcome this, recognize and challenge self-doubts and gradually build a more accurate self-view. As new behaviors become second nature, your self-esteem rises, and Imposter Syndrome naturally fades.

The Challenge of Advancing When People in Your Life Do Not

We expect our parents to be more advanced than we are. After all, this was the case when we were children. They seemed to have all the answers — guiding us through scraped knees, school struggles, and the complexities of growing up. But sometimes, children continue to grow and evolve while their parents remain firmly rooted in earlier stages of Personality Intelligence. This divergence can be a source of incredible frustration.

Conversations that once flowed effortlessly may become strained. The more advanced child yearns for connection but may feel misunderstood or invalidated. On the other hand, parents might feel bewildered or even rejected, struggling to comprehend why the child they once guided now challenges their perspectives.

This disconnect can often happen with siblings when one advances and the other does not. One sibling may embrace change, seeking personal development and exploring new behaviors. The other sibling, however, might remain firmly rooted in familiar ways of thinking and behaving. Whether due to fear, comfort, or a lack of desire for change, they may resist the growth that their sibling has embraced.

This imbalance can create tension. The evolving sibling may feel misunderstood, judged, or even dismissed. Conversations that once felt light and easy may now feel strained, as one sibling struggles to relate to the other's new perspectives. The unchanged sibling, in turn, may feel left behind or criticized, believing their sibling's growth is a rejection of their shared past. There can be resentment when growth is perceived as superiority or when one sibling's choices highlight the other's stagnation.

This pattern of growing beyond one's family can also take place with friends. Friendships often form during shared chapters of life, such as school years, first jobs, or common interests. In these moments, friendships can feel effortless, grounded in mutual understanding and a shared worldview.

But just as with family, personal growth can cause friends to grow apart. One friend may embark on a path of self-discovery, while the other may remain content within the familiar, holding on to past dynamics. At different levels of Personality Intelligence, they may no longer feel like they resonate with each other. This divergence can evoke complex emotions, especially if the individuals perceived that they would be friends for life.

Perhaps most challenging of all is facing the reality of dealing with a spouse when one has evolved and the other has not. People tend to form relationships with individuals at the same level of Personality Intelligence. This is especially true for our life partner. It would be surprising to see one spouse at Level 1 and the other at Level 3. But sometimes, one spouse evolves, and the other does not. This is a recipe for frustration and conflict, as the unevolved spouse can get under the skin of the person who has grown.

This occurs for a variety of reasons. First, lesser-evolved people reflect an old version of ourselves back to us, and we don't like it. The old behaviors remind us of who we were and chose not to be.

Second, the less evolved person can make the more evolved person fearful of regressing to a former state. Growth requires effort, and the individual who has progressed doesn't want their hard work to be undone.

Third, ironically, an individual who has transitioned to a higher level of Personality Intelligence may judge their partner for *not* growing. They might even be angry with them for not developing like they did. *I put in the work; why can't they?* the thinking goes.

Fourth, it's easier to change behavior than perception. Imagine an individual who, under pressure from their spouse, worked hard to transition from PIQ1 to PIQ2. Then, their spouse doesn't even notice the change.

I tested this premise many years ago by conducting a social experiment with my wife. Hey, no judgment! Here's what I did: We had a hamper in the corner of our bedroom for many years. At the end of the day, I did my best to throw my clothes into the hamper.

And by throw, I literally mean throw them from the other side of the room. Admittedly, sometimes I missed, and the clothes landed next to or in front of the hamper. In my Parrot mind, I was close, and close was good enough.

I assure you that close was *not* good enough for my Owl wife. She mentioned this to me periodically, so I endeavored to improve my aim. In retrospect, I should have just walked over to the hamper and placed it properly inside.

One year, as my New Year's Resolution, I committed to ensuring my clothes reached the hamper. I was dedicated to never leaving clothes on the floor again. And I did it, for an entire year. Despite my Parrot's daily desire to revel in my accomplishment, I didn't say a word about it until December 31.

To my dismay, after I shared my noteworthy achievement, my wife was surprised and did *not* share my celebratory mood. She swore that I still occasionally left clothes on the floor. At the risk of her reading this, I assure you, every item of clothing immediately made its way into the hamper.

Behavior change is hard, but noticing that others have changed is even harder. If one individual has advanced to the next level of Personality Intelligence, they may not notice their partner's growth. And that is a recipe for conflict.

So, what's the solution? If you've grown, but your partner hasn't, what can you do? The most important thing is to cultivate a mindset of acceptance rather than judgment. When you accept your partner fully, you create an environment of openness to learning. They are more likely to follow your lead and seek to grow if they do not feel judged.

In addition, no two people come together for the benefit of just one. Someone at a lower level of Personality Intelligence can help you develop an open heart if you are in a receptive space of unconditional regard.

It's not easy to progress from Level 1 to Level 4. If it were, everyone would do it. However, anyone dedicated to self-improvement can become the best version of themselves. You just have to want it, and you have to do the work.

Chapter 16:
Looking Forward

We all experience times of mastery when everything clicks, and we operate at our full potential. The key is recognizing these moments and striving to create more of them. Mastery isn't a permanent state but a collection of consistent, high-performing instances. What sets someone at Level 4 apart is their ability to generate these moments more frequently than someone in the earlier stages of development.

Mastery is about awareness, repetition, and deliberate practice. Each time you intentionally act as the Chameleon, you bolster your ability to function at that higher level. Over time, the accumulation of masterful moments raises your baseline performance.

Here are some closing tips for maximizing your Personality Intelligence:

- Look for the styles in your everyday life to develop your people-reading skills.

- Use your strengths, but don't overuse them.
- Embrace authenticity and be true to yourself.
- Consider the intentions of others, not just their behaviors.
- Take the time to reflect on who you are and how you affect the people in your life.
- Find someone who has mastered your style and emulate their behaviors.
- Ask, "What style is needed in this moment?" Then do that!

Ultimately, Personality Intelligence is about mastering the art of being fully, unapologetically, and authentically you. It's the quiet confidence of the Eagle soaring high, the vibrant Parrot energy helping others shine their light, the assertive Dove bringing peace and harmony, and the precise Owl who embraces life's ambiguities.

As you engage the power of being you, remember that true mastery is a journey from who you are to who you choose to become. Let this be your compass, guiding you not just to success but to a life of deep connection and purpose.

I'll see you on the path.

Epilogue

Time marched on, and Carter and Dawn had become senseis, each leading a school of their own. One day, they brought their students together to learn from each other. After the last student left the dojo, the old friends seized on the rare opportunity to spar with someone at their level. Without saying a word, they nodded and assumed fighting positions.

Meanwhile, a few students chatting outside the dojo noticed the action inside. Through the large bay window, they watched in awe, hardly believing their eyes. None of them had ever seen two masters sparring.

As the match began, the old friends stood opposite each other with calm, focused expressions. Their stances were perfectly balanced, and they moved with deliberate, almost meditative slowness, waiting for the ideal moment to strike. Each adjusted subtly—one shifting her foot, the other easing his shoulder back slightly. The students observed closely, captivated by the subtlety of their movements.

Out of nowhere, Dawn lightly touched her abdomen.

"What a minute!" said one of the new students. "What just happened?"

One of the white belts replied, "I think he just scored a point, but I didn't see anything. I mean, he didn't throw a punch. That makes no sense. Unless it was so fast that we all missed it."

They watched as the slow-motion battle waged on. Then it happened again. This time, Carter touched his side.

"I don't get it," lamented one of the newer students.

Suddenly, a black belt student's eyes grew wide. "I think I know what they're doing. They knew a point would have been scored based on their body positions, so they didn't throw the technique to prove it."

"He punched without punching?" the white belt asked.

"Not exactly," the black belt replied. "He was going to punch but didn't need to."

Another black belt added, "They've moved beyond technique. They no longer need to throw punches or kicks. They understand intention so profoundly, they know what the other is going to do before they do it."

They continued watching until the most senior black belt among them said, "It goes deeper than that. Years ago, Sensei once told me to punch with love. I wasn't ready to hear it, so it didn't make much sense at the time. But I think I'm beginning to understand. The senseis have devoted their lives to mastering the art of combat, honing the physical techniques along the way. Now, they have moved beyond the physical and are fully immersed in the art aspect of the martial arts, where every action is an expression of love and respect."

"I can see I have a long way to go," said one of the white belts. Although she wasn't entirely sure what all of this meant, she trusted that clarity would come with time.

Which Bird Are You?
Take the Assessment
and Find Out!

Millions of people around the world have taken DISC assessments. Note that I did not say *the* DISC Assessment. That's because there is no official DISC profile. Many organizations have a version of a DISC Profile, as the model is in the public domain. William Marston created the model in 1928 and never copyrighted it.

This means that there is no DISC oversight organization. There are no DISC police. Everyone can set their own standards, including how rigorously they validate their assessments. Some assessments are incredibly valid and reliable; others are not.

So, be careful. Validation studies are complicated and expensive. Anything scientifically validated will not be free. As with most things in life, you get what you pay for. If there's no validation study, it might be as accurate as the Facebook quiz that tells you which ice cream flavor is most like you.

My organization, Take Flight Learning, utilizes the *Taking Flight Profile*. This assessment has undergone rigorous validation testing and has been taken by more than fifteen million people—about twice the population of New Jersey. Over twenty-eight thousand people were in the validation study, a massive sample size for a study of this kind. In fact, the profile is periodically revalidated as words change meaning over time.

The profile includes information on each style's tendencies, desired environments, stress response, and improvement strategies. In addition to a full-page narrative description of your style, the report includes personalized information that describes your strengths, potential development areas, work style tendencies, needs/motivators, communication style, leadership style, approach to managing stress, navigating conflict, and more. The report contains tips for improvement and action-planning questions based on your style.

The *Taking Flight Profile* provides the foundation for increasing self-awareness, improving relationships, and getting better results.

You can purchase profiles at TakeFlightLearning.com.

Bibliography

Simone Biles

Apstein, S. "Simone Biles Is SI's 2024 Sportsperson of the Year," *Sports Illustrated*, December 15, 2024. https://www.si.com/sportsperson/simone-biles-sports-illustrated-2024-sportsperson-of-the-year

Biles, Simone, and Michelle Burford. *Courage to Soar: A Body in Motion, A Life in Balance.* Zondervan, 2016.

Burk, Rachelle. *The Story of Simone Biles: A Biography Book for New Readers.* Rockridge Press, 2020.

Burke, M. "'America hates me': Simone Biles opens up about overcoming 'twisties' and criticism ahead of Paris Olympics," *NBC News*, July 30, 2024. https://www.nbcnews.com/sports/olympics/simone-biles-paris-olympics-twisties-gymnastics-america-hates-me-rcna148139

Cash, M. "Simone Biles coached and cheered on her Team USA teammates after pulling out of the Olympics team all-around final," *Business Insider*, July 27, 2021. https://www.businessinsider.com/simone-biles-coached-cheered-on-teammates-after-team-final-withdrawal-2021-7

Gregorian, D. "'We have been failed': Simone Biles breaks down in tears recounting abuse by Larry Nassar," *NBC News*, September 15, 2021. https://www.nbcnews.com/politics/congress/we-have-been-failed-simone-biles-breaks-down-tears-recounting-n1279255

Guardian Sport. "'Haters hate it, so I love that even more': Simone Biles explains goat pendant backstory," *The Guardian,* August 1, 2024. https://www.theguardian.com/sport/article/2024/aug/01/simone-biles-goat-necklace-olympics-paris-2024

Miao, H. "Simone Biles credits therapy for her success at the Paris Olympics," *CNBC,* July 31, 2024. https://www.cnbc.com/2024/07/31/simone-biles-credits-therapy-for-her-success-at-the-paris-olympics.html

Miller, J. "All about gymnast Simone Biles' parents Nellie and Ron," *NBC Insider*, August 7, 2025. https://www.nbc.com/nbc-insider/simone-biles-parents-nellie-ron-adopted-photos

Newton, J. "Simone Biles tells 11 News what Paris Olympics means to her," *WBAL-TV*, August 12, 2024. https://www.wbaltv.com/article/simone-biles-interview-paris-olympic-games/61816891

Reneau, A. "Simone Biles' sweet gesture with younger gymnast has people praising the GOAT," *Upworthy*, June 15, 2021. https://www.upworthy.com/simone-biles-helps-teammate-fix-hair-as-mentor

Birds and Chameleons

Bergman, R. *Chameleons: Nature's Living Masterpieces.* Princeton University Press, 2011.

Clark, W. S., & Wheeler, B. K. *A Field Guide to the Raptors of Europe, the Middle East, and North Africa.* Oxford University Press, 2001.

Forshaw, J. M. *Parrots of the World.* Princeton University Press, 2010.

Konig, C., Weick, F., & Becking, J.-H. *Owls of the World*. Yale University Press, 2008.

Sibley, D. A. *The Sibley Guide to Birds*. Knopf, 2016.

Richard Branson

Branson, Richard. *Losing My Virginity: How I Survived, Had Fun, and Made a Fortune Doing Business My Way*. Crown Business, 2011.

Branson, Richard. *Screw It, Let's Do It: Lessons in Life and Business*. Virgin Books, 2006.

CNN, "Richard Branson: I was seen as the dumbest person in school," [Video] YouTube. August 22, 2024. https://www.youtube.com/watch?v=GeG_Dw4IuKo

Pressat Team. "Reliving 16 great PR stunts from Richard Branson," *Pressat*, August 15, 2014. https://pressat.co.uk/blog/2014/08/reliving-16-pr-stunts-from-richard-branson/

Rella, E. "'I enjoy life too much': Sir Richard Branson has an adventurous approach to business—but he never planned on being an entrepreneur," *Entrepreneur*, June 18, 2024. https://www.entrepreneur.com/living/how-richard-branson-grew-virgin-group-and-earned-billions/475131

Sylvester, R. "'Dyslexia is my superpower': How learning differently helped Richard Branson," *Robb Report*, July 19, 2022. https://robbreport.com.au/business/dyslexia-is-my-superpower-how-learning-differently-helped-richard-branson/

Sylvester, R. "Richard Branson: I was a school dropout and we're still killing creativity and risk," *The Times*, January 26, 2022. https://www.thetimes.com/uk/education/article/times-education-commission-richard-branson-i-was-a-school-dropout-and-we-re-still-killing-creativity-and-risk-5fc7jf66m

Wiener-Bronner, D. "How Richard Branson went from high-school dropout to billionaire," *CNN Business*. April 26, 2018. https://money.cnn.com/2018/04/26/news/companies/richard-branson-rebound/index.html

Chameleons in Various Cultures

Ellis, P. The *Celtic Guide to Myth and Magic*. Llewellyn Worldwide. 2001.

Graves, R. *The Greek Myths*. Penguin Books, 1955.

Harris, R. *Loki: The Trickster God of Norse Mythology*. CreateSpace, 2012.

Kowalewska, A. *Slavic Mythology: The Legends and Lore of Eastern Europe*. Skyhorse Publishing, 2018.

Narasimhan, M. *The Adventures of Hanuman*. Jaico Publishing, 2015.

Villalobos, R. *The Nahuales: Aztec Shapeshifters and Spiritual Guides*. University of Texas Press, 2001.

Neal deGrasse Tyson

Beard, A. "Life's Work: An Interview with Neil deGrasse Tyson" *Harvard Business Review*. January 2016. https://hbr.org/2016/01/neil-degrasse-tyson

Fernandez, R. "Why Neil deGrasse Tyson is Skeptical about Mars Colonization" *SlashGear*. May 2, 2022. https://www.slashgear.com/850556/why-neil-degrasse-tyson-is-skeptical-about-mars-colonization/

Maher, B. (Host), "Overtime: Neil deGrasse Tyson, Donna Brazile, Andrew Sullivan," [Video] *Real Time with Bill Maher*, YouTube. January 15, 2016. https://www.youtube.com/watch?v=WMzgXHhKarY

St. Petersburg College, "Dr. Neil deGrasse Tyson - Titanic 3D and Cameron "Wrong Sky." August 11, 2011. https://youtu.be/8B6jSfRuptY?si=D73yv85xzr7FwJj-

Tyson, N. D. *Letters from an Astrophysicist.* W.W. Norton & Company, 2019.

Tyson, N. D. *The Sky Is Not the Limit: Adventures of an Urban Astrophysicist.* W.W. Norton & Company, 2000.

Tyson, N. D. [@neildegrassetyson]. "The Universe is Under No Obligation to Make Sense to You" [Photograph] Instagram, August 10, 2023. https://www.instagram.com/p/Cvv_L9-Mctf/

Disorders

American Psychiatric Association. *Diagnostic and Statistical Manual of Mental Disorders (DSM-5) (5th ed.).* American Psychiatric Publishing, 2013.

Clarkin, J. F., & Levy, K. N. *Personality Disorders: Theories and Issues.* Guilford Press. 2004.

Gunderson, J. G., & Lyons, M. *Borderline Personality Disorder: A Clinical Guide.* American Psychiatric Publishing, 2008.

Kernberg, O. F. *Borderline Conditions and Pathological Narcissism.* Jason Aronson, 1975.

Miller, J. D., & Campbell, W. K. The *Narcissism Epidemic: Living in the Age of Entitlement.* Free Press, 2008.

Millon, T., Grossman, S., & Meagher, S. *Personality Disorders in Modern Life (2nd ed.).* Wiley, 2004.

O'Kearney, R., & Nunn, K. "Cognitive Behavioral Therapy for Obsessive-Compulsive Disorder: A Review of the Literature," *Clinical Psychology Review* 23, no. 4 (2003): 409–427.

Steketee, G., & Shafran, R. (Eds.). *Cognitive Behavioral Therapy for OCD: A Guide for Professionals.* Guilford Press, 2007.

Vaknin, S. *Malignant Self-Love: Narcissism Revisited.* Narcissus Publications, 2007.

Lady Gaga

Free the Slaves. "Lady Gaga's 'Bad Romance' video about… sex slavery?" *Free the Slaves*, September 13, 2010. https://freetheslaves.net/lady-gagas-bad-romance-video-about-sex-slavery/

Herbert, E. *Lady Gaga: Behind the Fame.* John Blake Publishing, 2010.

James, F. Lady Gaga's latest mental health update receives outpouring of support," *HELLO! Magazine,* September 6, 2023. https://www.hellomagazine.com/healthandbeauty/health-and-fitness/501834/lady-gagas-latest-mental-health-update-receives-outpouring-of-support/

Lady Gaga. Instagram, June 12, 2023. https://www.instagram.com/p/CtrwWbRPqTI/

Lester, P. *Lady Gaga: Looking for Fame: The Life of a Pop Princess.* Omnibus Press, 2010.

NFL, "Lady Gaga's FULL Pepsi Zero Sugar Super Bowl LI Halftime Show," [Video] YouTube. February 5, 2017. https://www.youtube.com/watch?v=txXwg712zw4

Reynolds, A. "Lady Gaga explains 'Disease' lyrics and music video meaning," *Capital FM*, October 30, 2024, https://www.capitalfm.com/news/music/lady-gaga-disease-lyrics-meaning/

Selena Gomez

Bailey, A. "Selena Gomez on why being seen as a 'victim' makes her 'so mad'," *ELLE*, November 2024. https://www.elle.com/culture/celebrities/a62965470/selena-gomez-victim-portrayal-thoughts/

D'Adamo, M. *Selena Gomez: The Ultimate Fan Book.* Independently published, 2017.

Donahue, A. "Emilia Pérez is a star-studded Oscars favourite, but it's also proving controversial," *ABC News*, January 20, 2025. https://www.abc.net.au/news/2025-01-20/emilia-perez-review-zoe-saldana-karla-sof%C3%ADa-gasc%C3%B3n-selena-gomez/104796886

Gomez, S. (2024, November 15). "Selena Gomez interview: 'Emilia Pérez,' music, and Disney," *The Hollywood Reporter*, November 15, 2024. https://www.hollywoodreporter.com/movies/movie-features/selena-gomez-interview-emilia-perez-music-disney-1236065885/

Henderson, C. "Selena Gomez and Eugenio Derbez respond to 'Emilia Pérez' criticism," *USA Today*, December 8, 2024. https://www.usatoday.com/story/entertainment/movies/2024/12/08/selena-gomez-eugenio-derbez-emilia-perez-criticism/76850708007/

James, S. *Selena Gomez: The Road to Success.* CreateSpace Independent Publishing Platform, 2021.

Lang, C. "Selena Gomez opens up about lupus and health journey," *Today*, September 10, 2024. https://www.today.com/health/mind-body/selena-gomez-lupus-health-rcna150374

Petruska, E. *Selena Gomez: Pop Star & Social Media Queen.* BookRix, 2015.

Wallace, F. (2016, August 31). "Selena Gomez has cancelled her Revival tour due to her mental health," *Vogue Australia*, August 31, 2016. https://www.vogue.com.au/celebrity/news/selena-gomez-has-cancelled-her-revival-tour-due-to-her-mental-health/news-story/85726509f7fab43a95bbdf12cfaf95d1

Introverts, Ambiverts, and Extroverts

Abele, A. E., & Wojciszke, B. *Personality and Social Psychology Bulletin*, 33 no. 2 (2007): 245–258.

Grant, A. *Give and Take: A Revolutionary Approach to Success.* Viking, 2013.

Hogan, J., Hogan, R., & Roberts, B. W. "Personality Measurement and Employment Decisions: Questions and Answers," *American Psychologist* 51, no. 5 (1996): 469–477.

Laney, M. *The Introvert Advantage: How to Thrive in an Extrovert World.* Workman Publishing, 2002.

McCrae, R. R., & Costa, P. T. *The Five-Factor Theory of Personality.* In O. P. John, R. W. Robins, & L. A. Pervin (Eds.), *Handbook of personality: Theory and research* (3rd ed., pp. 159–181). Guilford Press, 2008.

Schneider, T., & Jackson, D. "The Role of Ambiverts in Organizational Contexts: An Overview," *Journal of Organizational Behavior* 35, no. 5 (2014): 740–754.

Introverts and Depression

Nolen-Hoeksema, S., et al. *Rethinking Rumination.* Perspectives on Psychological Science, 2008.

Servaas, M. N., et al. *Neuroticism and the Brain.* Psychological Medicine, 2013.

Teo, A. R., et al. *Social isolation, loneliness, and all-cause mortality in older men and women.* Proceedings of the National Academy of Sciences, 2013.

Dwayne Johnson

Abdo, K. (2020). *Dwayne Johnson (WWE Superstars).* Abdo Zoom.

Dwayne "The Rock" Johnson shares his favorite quote. [video] YouTube. December 21, 2022. https://www.youtube.com/shorts/C8BmKaASNhU

Garcia, H. (2020). *The Rock: Through the lens: His life, his movies, his world*. St. Martin's Press.

Johnson, D., & Layden, J. (2000). *The Rock says...* HarperEntertainment.

William Marston

Lepore, J. *The Secret History of Wonder Woman*. Knopf, 2014.

Marston, W. M. *The Emotions of Normal People*. London: Kegan Paul, Trench, Trubner & Co., Ltd, 1928.

Neuroscience

Bear, M. F., Connors, B. W., & Paradiso, M. A. *Neuroscience: Exploring the Brain (4th ed.)*. Lippincott Williams & Wilkins, 2015.

Cacioppo, J. T., & Patrick, W. *Loneliness: Human Nature and the Need for Social Connection*. W.W. Norton & Company, 2008.

Gray, J. A. *Brain Systems and the Biological Bases of Personality*. In L. A. Pervin (Ed.),

Handbook of Personality: Theory and Research (pp. 244–276). Guilford Press, 1990.

Lieberman, M. D. *Social: Why Our Brains Are Wired to Connect*. Crown Publishing, 2013.

Nussbaum, M. (2016). "Neuroscience and the Well-Being of Human Nature," *Personality and Social Psychology Review* 20, no. 3 (2016): 180–189.

Optimism

Carver, C. S., Scheier, M. F., & Segerstrom, S. C. "Optimism," *Clinical Psychology Review* 30, no. 7 (2010): 879–889.

Lee, L. O., James, P., Zevon, E. S., Kim, E. S., Trudel-Fitzgerald, C., Spiro, A., & Kubzansky, L. D. "Optimism is Associated with Exceptional Longevity in 2 Epidemiologic Cohorts of Men and Women," *Proceedings of the National Academy of Sciences* 116, no. 37 (2019): 18357–18362.

Rasmussen, H. N., Scheier, M. F., & Greenhouse, J. B. "Optimism and Physical Health: A Meta-Analytic Review," *Annals of Behavioral Medicine* 37, no. 3 (2009): 239–256.

Personality

American Psychological Association. (n.d.) *Personality*. In *APA Dictionary of Psychology*. https://dictionary.apa.org/personality

Keanu Reeves

CBS, "What do you think will happen when we die Keanu Reeves?" [Video] YouTube. May 10, 2019. https://youtu.be/cGFSh6Cis-s

Dosani, R. "'Gorgeous things' Keanu Reeves has done for people," *Metro*, April 16, 2024. https://metro.co.uk/2024/04/16/gorgeous-things-keanu-reeves-done-people-20660150/

Doyle, W. *Keanu Reeves: A Life.* St. Martin's Press, 2021.

Fleming, D. *Keanu Reeves: A Spiritual Journey.* Rowman & Littlefield, 2018.

icönik. "The Life of Keanu Reeves: A Journey of Resilience, Kindness, and Success," *icönik* magazine, November 15, 2024. https://www.iconikmagazine.com/post/the-life-of-keanu-reeves-a-journey-of-resilience-kindness-and-success

The New Zealand Herald, "Best of 2019: Tragic true story of Keanu Reeves' tough life and why the world is embracing him *The New Zealand Herald*, December 28, 2019. https://tinyurl.com/5dstn4c3

Torres, L. "15 reasons fans believe Keanu Reeves is the greatest person ever," *Business Insider*, August 22, 2019. https://www.businessinsider.com/keanu-reeves-greatest-person-ever-2019-8

Virgin Radio. "Here are some of Keanu Reeves' acts of kindness as he celebrates his 58th birthday," Virgin Radio UK, September 2, 2022. https://virginradio.co.uk/entertainment/74095/here-are-some-of-keanu-reeves-acts-of-kindness-as-he-celebrates-his-58th-birthday

Arnold Schwarzenegger

Rella, E. "Arnold Schwarzenegger at University of Houston Commencement: 'None of Us Can Make It Alone'," *TIME*, May 15, 2017. https://time.com/4779796/arnold-schwarzenegger-university-of-houston-uh-commencement-graduation/

Schwarzenegger, A. "Ask Arnold," *Schwarzenegger.com*, 2021. https://web.archive.org/web/20080523203926/http://www.schwarzenegger.com/en/news/askarnold/news_askarnold_eng_legacy_444.asp?sec=news&subsec=askarnold

Schwarzenegger, Arnold. *Be Useful: Seven Tools for Life*. Penguin Press, 2023.

Schwarzenegger, A. [@schwarzenegger]. "Congrats to all the @UHouston grads! Thank you for letting me be part of your big day..." Instagram, May 15, 2017. https://www.instagram.com/p/BUAaH9JgWvv/

Schwarzenegger, Arnold, & Petre, P. *Total Recall: My Unbelievably True-Life Story*. Simon & Schuster, 2012.

Roger Sperry

Sperry, R. W. "The Divided Brain: The Biology of Brain and Behavior," *Science* 185, no. 4156 (1974): 347–355.

Sperry, R. W. *Hemispheric Specialization and the Unity of Consciousness.* In P. E. Vernon (Ed.), Brain Mechanisms and Consciousness (pp. 123–134). Springer, 1968.

Sperry, R. W. "Some Applications of the Split-brain Paradigm to Cognitive and Behavioral Functioning," *Science* 213, no. 4503 (1981): 47–52.

Michael Strahan

ABC News. "'GMA' co-anchor Michael Strahan to fly to space on Blue Origin's next space flight," *ABC News*, November 23, 2021. https://abcnews.go.com/GMA/Culture/gma-anchor-michael-strahan-fly-space-blue-origins/story?id=81339655

ABC News. "Kelly Ripa and Michael Strahan's best costumes ever," *ABC News*, 2013. https://abcnews.go.com/Entertainment/photos/kelly-ripa-michael-strahans-best-costumes-20719772

ABC News, "Michael Strahan's space liftoff" [Video] YouTube. December 11, 2021. https://www.youtube.com/watch?v=LQuGznlh2y8

Chang, A. "Jeff Bezos' Blue Origin poised to send former NFL player Michael Strahan into space," *Los Angeles Times*, December 11, 2021. https://www.latimes.com/business/story/2021-12-11/jeff-bezos-blue-origin-poised-to-send-former-nfl-player-michael-strahan-into-space

Strahan, Michael, and Jay Glazer. *Inside the Helmet: My Life as a Sunday Afternoon Warrior.* Gotham Books, 2007.

The Week Staff. "Bezos Launches Michael Strahan into Space," *The Week*, December 11, 2021. https://theweek.com/space/1007984/bezos-launches-michael-strahan-into-space

Style and Type Systems

Black Elk, N., & Brown, H. *The Sacred Hoop of the Lakota: Spiritual Wisdom from the Heart of the Native American Tradition*. Bear & Company, 2000.

Desy, P. L. *4 Spirit Keepers of the Native American Medicine Wheel*. Learn Religions, 2024.

Knafo, D. "The Four Temperaments and Their Relevance in Contemporary Psychology," *Journal of Personality Psychology* 21, no. 3 (2014): 230–245.

Qu, L. *The Dao of Personality: Using Chinese Medicine to Explore Your Nature*. Beijing University Press, 2012.

Stanton, A. *The Four Temperaments: An Overview of Hippocrates' Theory*. Psychology Press, 2018.

Witztum, E., & Schlesinger, M. "Temperament and Character: Historical Perspectives from Hippocrates to Modern Theory," *Journal of Psychological Research* 59, no. 4 (2006): 314–328.

Sweat Lodges

Adler, Judith. *Cleansing the Body, Cleansing the Soul: The Ritual Use of Steam and Sweat in Ancient and Modern Societies*. University Press of America, 2002.

Jensen, Dianne. *Sweat Lodge: The Way to Purification*. Element Books, 1998.

Kaaber, Håkon. *Sauna, Sweat and Steam: A Global History of Bathing*. Amberley Publishing, 2023.

Werness, Hope B. *Sweat Bathing: The Finnish Sauna, Russian Banya, and Native American Sweat Lodge*. McFarland & Company, 2021.

Taylor Swift

Dalley, H. "Taylor Swift's piano malfunction reaction during Eras Tour," *Billboard*, June 24, 2023. https://www.billboard.com/music/music-news/taylor-swift-piano-malfunction-reaction-eras-tour-1235333657/

Dalley, H. and Aniftos, R. "A Timeline of Taylor Swift's Generosity," *Billboard*, January 17, 2025.https://www.billboard.com/lists/taylor-swifts-charity-donations-gifts-timeline/

Dalley, H. and Spruch, K. "Taylor Swift & Scooter Braun's Feud: A Timeline," *Billboard*, October 25, 2024. https://tinyurl.com/5cdcucyj

Grady, C. "Why Taylor Swift is rerecording all her old songs," *Vox*, February 12, 2021. https://www.vox.com/culture/22278732/taylor-swift-re-recording-1989-speak-now-enchanted-mine-master-rights-scooter-braun

Schneider, Marc. "Taylor Swift Buys Back Her Masters From Shamrock, Reclaiming Her First Six Albums," Billboard, May 30, 2025. https://www.billboard.com/pro/taylor-swift-regains-control-master-recordings-shamrock/

Wenner, Jody. *The Biography of Taylor Swift: A Comprehensive Biography.* Independently published, 2023.

Trait Theory

Allport, G. W. *Personality: A Psychological Interpretation.* Holt, 1937.

Cattell, R. B. "The Description of Personality: Basic Traits Revealed in Man's Descriptions of Himself," *Journal of Abnormal and Social Psychology* 38, no. 4 (1943): 476506.

Roberts, B. W., & Jackson, J. J. "The Personality-Related Situational Strength Context Model: A Comprehensive Review of Trait Theory," *Annual Review of Psychology*, 69 (2018): 427–447.

Type A and Type B

Friedman, M., & Rosenman, R. H. *Type A Behavior and Your Heart.* Knopf, 1974.

Williams, R. L., & Mott, L. A. "Type A and Type B Behavior Patterns: Effects on Stress, Cardiovascular Health, and Coping Mechanisms," *Journal of Behavioral Medicine* 13, no. 2 (1990): 115–131.

Type Theory

Jung, C. G. *Psychological Types.* Routledge, 1921.

Nettle, D. *Personality: What Makes You the Way You Are.* Oxford University Press, 2007.

Thompson, R. C. (1982). "Type and Trait Theory: A Comparison of Jungian Typology and Trait Personality Theory," *Journal of Personality Assessment* 46, no. 6 (1982): 614–619.

Emma Watson

Battison, K. (2024, September 30). "Emma Watson addressed why she keeps rejecting Hollywood roles as she approaches six years since last film," *LADbible*, September 30, 2024. https://www.ladbible.com/entertainment/film/emma-watson-rejecting-hollywood-film-roles-why-901271-20240930

Burke, O. "Emma Watson explains why we don't see her in films anymore after feeling 'caged'," *LADbible*, December 20, 223. https://www.ladbible.com/entertainment/celebrity/emma-watson-why-no-films-acting-001438-20231220

Giannini, A. "How Emma Watson's Belle differs from the character in the original 'Beauty and the Beast'," *Business Insider*, March 6, 2017. https://www.businessinsider.com/emma-watsons-belle-differs-from-original-2017-3

O'Malley, K. (2017, February 14). "Emma Watson went to princess bootcamp for 'Beauty and the Beast,'" *ELLE UK*, February 14, 2017. https://www.elle.com/uk/life-and-culture/culture/news/a35475/ emma-watson-went-to-princess-bootcamp-beauty-and-the-beast-belle/

Warner Bros., "Emma Watson's Harry Potter Outtake," [Video] YouTube. July 15, 2011. https://www.youtube.com/ watch?v=bxMiLwA3qQ4

Watson, E. *Our Shared Shelf: The Feminist Book Club.* 2016.

Weldon, F. *Emma Watson: An Inspiring Role Model.* Hachette Books, 2014.

About the Author

Merrick Rosenberg, affectionately known as The Bird Guy, is not just an author, keynote speaker, and entrepreneur. He's a true visionary! In 1991, he founded Team Builders Plus, one of the first team-building companies in the United States. His groundbreaking work laid the foundation for the team-building industry we know today.

But Merrick didn't stop there! After transforming the lives of hundreds of thousands by creating positive work environments, he took his mission a step further by connecting classic DISC styles to the Eagle, Parrot, Dove, and Owl. In 2012, he launched his second venture, Take Flight Learning, to share these insights with the world.

His impressive client roster includes two-thirds of the Fortune 100 companies, showcasing his expertise across small, mid-sized, and large organizations, non-profits, and government agencies. He's penned eight award-winning books, including *The*

Chameleon, *Which Bird Are You?*, and *Personality Wins*, enabling individuals to harness the power of their personality.

Merrick is also an acclaimed filmmaker. His personality styles movie, *BirdBrains, Inc.*, has won an astounding twenty-three film festival awards, including multiple honors for *Best Short Film*, *Best Original Song*, and *Best Educational Film*. If you haven't seen it, go watch it today! And good luck getting the song, "Personality," out of your head.

Armed with an MBA in Organizational Development from Drexel University, where he was honored as *Alumni Entrepreneur of the Year*, Merrick's accolades don't end there. He's been recognized as *New Jersey CEO of the Year* by *AI magazine* and *Delaware Valley HR Consultant of the Year* by the Society for Human Resource Management.

Merrick not only understands how to grow a business but also knows how to create an organization where people love to work. Under his leadership, Take Flight Learning was named *New Jersey Business of the Year* by *NJ Biz magazine* and recognized by the *Philadelphia Business Journal* as one of the *Fastest Growing Companies* and *Best Places to Work* in the region.

Merrick captivates audiences at major conferences and events, including TEDx, the Society for Human Resource Management, the Association for Talent Development, Vistage International, Commercial Real Estate Women, the Project Management Institute, the International Society for Performance Improvement, the Young Associates, and countless others.

He's also a sought-after media guest, gracing the airwaves of ABC, NBC, CBS, PBS, SiriusXM, iHeart Radio, and Radio Disney, with interviews in prestigious publications like the *New York Times*, *Fortune*, the *Wall Street Journal*, *Forbes*, *Newsweek*, *Fast Company*, *Inc.*, *Parents*, and *Glamour*.

And when he's not inspiring people to be their best selves, you might find Merrick unwinding in a yoga studio, meditating on a serene beach, or strumming his guitar with friends.

Learn more about Merrick's books
and speaking engagements at:
MerrickRosenberg.com.

About Team Builders Plus and Take Flight Learning

In 1991, Merrick Rosenberg and Jeff Backal launched Team Builders Plus, one of the world's first team-building companies. Their creative and transformative programs didn't just engage, but they also set the stage for today's team-building industry. Team Builders Plus offers the full range of team-building programs, including team-bonding events, philanthropic activities, and developmental sessions.

By 1994, they observed a common issue in many workplaces: conflict frequently arose from people failing to understand each other's needs. Team members and managers needed a way to communicate effectively with all types of people, and companies realized that fostering a positive work environment was vital to retaining talent. By weaving the interactive energy of team building into DISC training, Team Builders Plus became a leader in DISC-based programs across the US.

Then, in 2012, Merrick Rosenberg reinvented the DISC model in his book *Taking Flight!* as he linked the styles to Eagles, Parrots, Doves, and Owls. With this fresh, memorable approach, Take Flight Learning was born.

Here's where it got interesting. Rather than one-and-done training programs, Take Flight Learning created an ecosystem of programs, profiles, products, and services built around the four styles. It didn't take long before they noticed the styles becoming embedded into the organizational culture.

Their flagship *Taking Flight with DISC* program guides people to understand and apply the styles throughout their lives. But we know learning doesn't stop with one session. After the first program, individuals can deepen their knowledge in *Taking Flight with EQ*, *Innovating IDEAs*, and *ReDISCovering Conflict*. Teams can learn how to improve their culture with *Team Dynamics*. Leaders can learn how to integrate the styles into how they manage and lead others through *Chameleon Leadership*, and salespeople can learn how to incorporate the styles into the sales process through *Chameleon Selling*. In addition, coaches can learn how to build the styles into every coaching interaction.

If you want to reinforce style wisdom further, try self-paced learning through the gamified eLearning in Style.

Take Flight Learning can lead sessions for you, or you can get certified to deliver your own style-based programs. The certifications are hands-on and dynamic, going far beyond basic graphs. You'll get everything you need—PowerPoint decks, guides, desktop birds, and more—to be an outstanding trainer.

Discover a variety of team building programs at
TeamBuildersPlus.com.

Learn how to bring the styles into your company at
TakeFlightLearning.com.

See the birds come to life at
BirdBrainsInc.com.

TAKING FLIGHT
WITH DISC

TEAM
DYNAMICS

CHAMELEON
LEADERSHIP

TAKING FLIGHT WITH
EQ

CHA
MEL
EON
CHAMELEON
SELLING

Coaching
in Style

reDISCovering
Conflict

reDISCovering
Conflict

INNOVATING
IDEAS

BirdBrains, Inc.

www.ingramcontent.com/pod-product-compliance
Lightning Source LLC
Chambersburg PA
CBHW051134120626
46547CB00012B/796